# CUSTOMS AND CEREMONIES

Would you like to scramble for hot pennies, see Saint George kill the dragon, dance in the streets to a steel band, or watch a Viking longboat go up in flames? These are just some of the exciting customs and ceremonies described in this book.

# CUSTOMS AND CEREMONIES

## Elizabeth Holt and Molly Perham
## Illustrated by ross

Evans Brothers Limited London

© 1980 Elizabeth Holt and Molly Perham
Illustrations © 1980 Evans Brothers Limited

First published 1980 by Evans Brothers Limited,
Montague House, Russell Square, London WC1B 5BX.

All Rights Reserved. No part of this publication
may be reproduced, stored in a retrieval system, or
transmitted, in any form, or by any means, electronic,
mechanical, photocopying, recording or otherwise, without
the prior permission of Evans Brothers Limited.

British Library Cataloguing in Publication Data

Holt, Elizabeth
    Customs and ceremonies. — (Activities nationwide).
    1. Great Britain — Social life and customs —
    20th century — Juvenile literature
    I. Title  II. Perham, Molly  III. Series
    390'.0941    DA566.4

    ISBN 0-237-45507-2

PRA 6841
Printed and bound in Great Britain by
William Clowes (Beccles) Limited
Beccles and London

# Contents

| | |
|---|---:|
| January | 1 |
| February | 8 |
| March | 18 |
| April | 28 |
| May | 31 |
| June | 47 |
| July | 58 |
| August | 64 |
| September | 70 |
| October | 75 |
| November | 79 |
| December | 84 |
| Notes | 90 |
| Index | 95 |

# About This Book

Almost every day of every year some sort of custom or ceremony takes place in Great Britain. We haven't been able to include all of them, but have selected the most interesting and entertaining. As far as we have been able to check, those we have mentioned are still carried on, but while some survive as they always have done, others change and some, sadly, die.

However, as people from other countries have settled here, so they have brought their own customs and traditions to enrich our cultural life — and we have included some of these fascinating and colourful ceremonies.

Many customs are described as moveable feasts. This simply means that they do not come on the same calendar day each year — they are dependent upon the moon.

If you know of a particularly interesting custom in your area, we would love to hear about it. Or, if we have some detail wrong, we would like to hear about that, too. Should you particularly want to see one of the customs we have described, it is advisable to check with the local British Tourist Authority office, or the local town hall, to make sure that the event really is going to take place. We wouldn't want you to make a long journey and be disappointed.

Happy Wassailing!

# January

*January 1st*
**First-footing**
Although many New Year's Eve celebrations continue into New Year's Day, first-footing, a custom kept up particularly in Scotland and Northern England, is really the first one of the year.

Now, whether you'll be a welcome first-footer or not depends upon your appearance. Women are out. They are considered unlucky practically everywhere. Even if you are a man it's just bad luck if you are flat-footed, cross-eyed, or have thick eyebrows that meet in the middle. You won't be wanted either, and only in a few regions like parts of Scotland and West Yorkshire will red-haired people be looked on favourably. On the other hand, if you are young, healthy, good-looking and male, you'll be welcomed with open arms.

The way that a first-footer arrives is very important. He should knock and come in by the front door carrying a small piece of coal or peat, money, bread and salt, for these are all tokens of prosperity for the coming year. In some places he should enter silently and no one should speak until he has placed the coal or the peat on the fire, but in others he is supposed to greet the family loudly and be welcomed warmly in return.

Although we think of first-footing as a British custom, it's one that is carried on in many parts of Europe too.

*January: moveable*
## Chinese New Year
The Chinese date the New Year from the first day of the first month of the lunar calendar. During this fifteen-day festival friends and relatives visit each other, debts are paid, gifts are exchanged and the children are given lucky money in red envelopes.

In the Chinese quarter in London the streets are filled with people celebrating. There are elaborate floats, dragons, music and dancing. Every now and again firecrackers are set off to greet the spirits.

*January 5th*
## Cutting of the Baddeley Cake
**London: Theatre Royal**
Robert Baddeley used to be a chef, but he managed to leave the kitchen and go on the stage. He became a very successful actor and so, when he died in 1794, he left a bequest of £100 to be used to provide wine and a cake to be shared between the actors performing in theatre on this day. The cake is carried with great ceremony into the Green

Room and there the actors toast Robert Baddeley and then munch their way through the cake.

## January 6th
### Royal Epiphany
### London: Chapel Royal, St James's Palace

This ceremony, which commemorates the arrival of the three kings to see the infant Jesus, usually takes place at 11.30 am and is open to the public. Splendidly dressed Gentlemen Ushers offer the traditional gifts of gold, frankincense and myrrh on behalf of the Queen. Silk bags containing the gifts are placed on an elaborate plate and taken up to the altar. Later the gold, which actually consists of twenty-five sovereigns, is changed into today's money and distributed to the aged poor.

## January 6th
### Throwing the Hood
### Haxey, Lincolnshire

This goes back to the 13th century when Lady de Mowbray was riding to church. A gust of wind blew off her scarlet hood, and thirteen villagers rushed to pick it up for her. In gratitude she donated a piece of land, still called Hoodland, and said that the rent from it should be used to provide a leather hood to be competed for by the villagers each year. It still is.

The game is organized by King Boggan, his attendants and the Fool. King Boggan, who wears a tall hat and carries a staff made from willow wands, arrives at 2 pm. The old story of the hood is told by the Fool, and then he is smoked — that is, the paper streamers that cascade down his back are set alight — and off everyone goes to Haxey Hill.

Twelve canvas hoods are thrown up. Anyone who manages to reach a village inn without being caught gets a small sum of money. Once these have been competed for, a last hood, this time a leather one, is tossed up and the Sway begins. The hill becomes a heaving, sweating mass of people, all pushing and shoving as they try to grab hold of the hood. Finally, once the hood has reached a pub which then becomes its home until the following year, there are much-needed drinks all round.

*January 6th: following Monday*
**Plough Monday**
This is the first Monday following the twelve days of
Christmas. Spring ploughing was supposed to start immediately
the fun of Christmas was over, but actually it became an
extra day of junketing. Young men decorated their ploughs,
dragged them around the village, and then took them to
church for blessing. One particular plough called the Fool
Plough used to go up and down streets accompanied by men
dressed up and with blackened faces. In some places the
ploughmen performed a play or danced, but in others they
just demanded food and drink. Everyone paid up. If they
didn't there was a good chance that the ground in front of
their houses would be ploughed up.

Today, instead of celebrating Plough Monday, many
churches have a Plough Sunday service.

*January 6th: following Monday*
**Plough Stots Service**
Goathland Village, North Yorkshire
The name for this custom comes from 'stot', the old name
for a bullock. This became the name for the young men who
dragged the plough around on Plough Monday.

Today there are three sets of dancers each carrying 76
centimetre (30 inch) long steel swords. The dances they
perform are believed to be Scandinavian and were brought
here by Norsemen more than a thousand years ago.

*January 6th: following Thursday*
**Jankyn Smith's Dole**
Bury St Edmund's, Suffolk
In the 18th century Jankyn Smith built almshouses and
provided the money for two chancel aisles in St Mary's
church. He asked that there should be a special service in
his memory. It is still given. After it the poor are given a
small sum of money and the very last coin is given to the
verger.

Thomas Bright must have thought this was a good idea
because he added to the occasion by leaving a bequest so
that cakes and ale could be provided at Jankyn Smith's
service. Nowadays it's the trustees who enjoy sherry and cake.

*January 6th and 7th*
**Russian Orthodox Christmas**
These are the two days when members of the Russian Orthodox Church celebrate Christmas Eve and Christmas Day. Right up to the 4th century these were the dates when Christmas Day and Christmas Eve were celebrated in Britain.

*January 11th*
**Burning the Clavie**
**Burghead, Grampian**
This impressive ceremony takes place on old New Year's Eve. In the afternoon young men, supervised by the Clavie King, make the Clavie, a kind of wooden basket on a long pole, filled with inflammable materials. This has to be done in a special way. No stranger may help or even handle the tools, and everything used must be given or borrowed — nothing must be bought.

At dusk the Clavie King lights the Clavie with peat from a fire which is already burning. The Clavie is lifted high, and the procession starts off, winding its way through the streets of the old town, and here and there people rush to pick up any bits that fall from the burning Clavie. Every now and again, as the heat from the burning Clavie becomes unbearable, someone else shoulders the burden — to drop it would bring bad luck. Finally it reaches a hill and here it is slotted into a kind of stone pillar. When the Clavie is finally broken up, small pieces of it, some still glowing, roll down the hill, and everyone scrambles for a bit of it so that they will have good luck throughout the coming year.

This custom might have developed from the time when fishermen circled round boats in the harbour with flaming torches. This kept away witches who were particularly nasty to fishermen. *See* The Old Calendar, p 93.

*January 17th*
**Wassailing the Apple Tree**
**Carhampton, Somerset**
To wassail someone is to drink their health. Down in the West Country the health of the orchard is drunk, usually on Old Twelfth Night. These orchards are important since the apples are used to make cider, and it's worth taking a bit

of trouble over them. People stand in a circle round the largest tree singing:

> *Old apple tree, old apple tree,*
> *We've come to wassail thee.*

A shot gun is fired to drive away any evil spirits that are lurking about, cider is thrown on the trunk of the tree, and pieces of cider-soaked cake or toast are hung on the branches, and the tree is toasted in cider. Everyone goes off confidently, sure that the orchard will do well in the coming year. By the way, the cake and toast are really for robins as they are lucky birds. *See* The Old Calendar, p 93.

*January 17th*
**Wassailing the Apple Tree**
**Roadwater, Somerset**
A similar ceremony is performed here, but when it's over the men pop into the local inn. That's normal enough, you might think, but the curious thing is that they enter by the back door, drink the health of the house, and leave by the back door. To go in and out the other way round might undo all the good that had been done to the trees by the wassailing.

*January: moveable*
**Swami Vivekananda's Birthday**
On this day Hindus remember their great reformer and leader.

*January 30th*
**Commemoration of the death of Charles I**
**London: Trafalgar Square**
On January 30th, 1649, King Charles I was executed in front of a large crowd. Some people still regard him as a martyr, and so a wreath is laid at the foot of his statue in Trafalgar Square on the Whitehall side, and a service of commemoration is held. If you later walk down Whitehall to the Banqueting Hall, you'll see that a wreath has been placed there too, for this is where the execution actually took place.

*January 31st*
**Dicing for the Maids' Money**
**Guildford, Surrey**
When John How died in 1674, he left a bequest. The interest on the money he left had to be diced for by two maids who had been servants in Guildford for at least two years. However, they couldn't enter the contest if they worked either in an inn or an alehouse. The girl who threw the highest number won the prize.

However, John How's charity became mixed up with another and so, curiously enough, the winner receives less money than the loser.

This custom still takes place at the Guild Hall.

*January: last Tuesday*
**Up-Helly-Aa**
**Lerwick, Shetland**
This fantastic fire festival goes back to the time when dead Viking chiefs were sent to their heaven, Valhalla, in their own blazing ships.

The Chief Guiser, the organizer, who is helped by hundreds of other Guisers, constructs a marvellous Viking ship, about 9 metres (30 feet) long and complete with oars and decorated shields.

In the early evening the galley is brought to the starting point where a huge procession of men dressed magnificently as Vikings has drawn up. With blazing torches held aloft, they wait the arrival of Guiser Jarl. Dressed in Viking armour, he takes the helm of the galley, and they move off. Bands play, the torches flicker, and the Guisers stride out.

When they reach the burning site, a circle is formed round the ship, and the torches are tossed in. As it blazes spectacularly, everyone sings the *Norseman's Home*. As the ship burns, everyone begins dancing and singing, and each group of Guisers goes to each one of the thirteen Lerwick Halls for even more celebrations. In fact, the town echoes with music throughout most of the night.

*January: moveable*
**Guru Gobind Singh's Birthday**
Sikhs come from India, many of them from the Punjab.

Sikhism was founded by Nanak who lived from 1469-1533. Its basis is the Unity of God and the Brotherhood of Man. After Nanak's death he was followed as Guru, the chief priest, by other rulers. Guru Gobind Singh, whose birthday is celebrated by special services in temples, instituted the Brotherhood of the Faithful, the Singhs. The Singhs wear long hair, a comb, a sword, long drawers and a steel bracelet. Gobind Singh was assassinated in 1708 and since then the Granth Sahib, the holy book of the Sikhs, has taken the place of a leader.

# February

*February 2nd*
**Candlemas**
A number of Christian customs take place on February 2nd. When benefactors left money or the money to buy goods for the poor, they usually stipulated that gifts should be handed over either on the anniversary of their death or on the day of an important church festival, and frequently Candlemas was chosen.

Candlemas commemorates the day when Jesus was first taken to the Temple, and it is also the day when, in many churches, candles are blessed, distributed, and then carried in procession.

This is probably a carry-over from Lupercalia, a Roman festival, and of another old Christian festival when people marched round the streets carrying flaming torches.

*February 2nd*
**Forty Shilling Day**
**Wotton, Surrey**
Five boys in Wotton can each win the equivalent of forty shillings, provided they can meet the conditions set down in William Glanville's will in 1717. Mind you, it's not that easy to earn the money. The boys have to go to his tomb, lay their hands on it and, without any help, recite the Lord's Prayer, the Apostle's Creed and the Ten Commandments. Then they

have to read the 13th chapter of Corinthians aloud and write out two verses in a clear and legible hand.

Sometimes this curious custom takes place later in the month if the weather is really awful, for William Glanville's tomb is outside in the churchyard. I don't suppose the boys mind. It gives them a bit longer to practise.

*February 2nd*
**Bread Dole**
**Woodbridge, Suffolk**
When George Carlow died in 1738 he made sure that he would be remembered by leaving money so that bread could be distributed from his gravestone to needy people.

*February 2nd*
**Handball**
**Jedburgh, Borders**
This is a wild game of handball played with leather balls decorated with coloured streamers which starts at 2 pm at the Cross. Since the pitch is the town streets, prudent people protect their windows and shut up their shops. The goals are at Castle Hill and Townfoot, and the teams are called Uppies and Downies, depending on which side of the Mercat Cross they were born.

The game goes on for hours with tussles in the streets, gardens and, sometimes, in the River Jed. The balls can be tossed, run with, smuggled from hand to hand, but they mustn't be kicked. Some people think that the game commemorates the Scots' victory over the English when the heads of Englishmen killed in battle were tossed around the town — authentic or not, it's a good story.

Another game takes place later on, but the date varies. Officially it takes place on the first Tuesday after the new moon following Candlemas, but it often takes place on Shrove Tuesday, a traditional day for wild games of football.

*February 2nd (or Sunday nearest)*
**Rocking Ceremony**
**Blidworth, Nottingham**
This is a charming Christian ceremony which commemorates the presentation of Jesus in the Temple. An old wooden cradle

decorated with greenery and flowers is brought into the church and placed in the candle-lit chancel. The boy in the parish who was born nearest to Christmas Day is christened at the Eucharist service at 9.30 am. Later the baby is placed in the cradle and gently rocked.

*February: moveable*
**Tu B'shvat**

The Jews had a very nice custom when babies were born. If the baby was a girl, a cypress tree was planted, and if it was a boy, they planted a cedar tree. When the children grew up and married, these trees were cut down and the wood was used to make a marriage canopy.

Today some children in Jewish Schools collect money and this is used to plant trees in Israel.

*February: moveable*
**Prophet Muhammad's Birthday**
This is an important day for Muslims who tell each other stories about the life and work of the Prophet. The founder of the Muslim faith was born in Mecca and, after years of meditation and secret teaching, he proclaimed himself the prophet of God. The basis of this faith is the Koran, a sacred work which Muhammad dictated to scribes whilst in a trance.

*February 3rd*
**Blessing of Throats**
**London: St Ethelreda, Ely Place**
If you have a sore throat or any infection of the throat, then St Ethelreda's is the place to go. Candles are blessed and dedicated to St Blaise, and then they are tied together with ribbons. The sick person kneels before the altar and the candles are then placed on the throat. The priest says, 'May the Lord deliver you from the evil of the throat, and free from every other evil.' The blessings take place every half hour from 8 am to 8 pm.

This used to be a holiday for those who worked in wool manufacturing since St Blaise was the patron saint of wool-combers. Poor St Blaise died horribly. He first had his flesh ripped to pieces with sharp iron combs, and then he was beheaded.

*February: Monday following the first Sunday after 3rd*
**Hurling the Silver Ball**
**St Ives, Cornwall**
This game takes place on Feasten Monday, the day after Feasten Sunday, because that's the day that St Ian, the patron saint of St Ives, arrived in Cornwall from Ireland, on her personal form of transport — a leaf.

Hurling used to be the most popular game in Cornwall. In this case the ball, which is about the size of a tennis ball, is made of wood and covered with silver leaf. At 10.30 am the Mayor throws the ball and then it is passed or tossed from hand to hand. As the church clock chimes at midday the person holding the ball takes it along to the Mayor at the Guildhall and gets the reward of 25p.

*February 14th*
**St Valentine's Day**
This is the day when young men send Valentine cards to the girls they love, or would like to have as girlfriends. St Valentine was a priest who was put to death for his faith by the Roman Emperor Claudius II during the 3rd century A.D. He was known as the 'apostle of true love' because he secretly performed the marriage ceremony for soldiers, who were forbidden by Claudius to marry. When

he was thrown into jail he fell in love with the jailer's daughter, and on the day he was put to death he left a little note for her signed 'Your Valentine'.

Perhaps Valentine was allocated February 14th as a Saint's Day because the pre-Christian Roman festival of Lupercalia was on February 15th — on that day young men chose a girl by a sort of lottery system. The girl could not be sure which boy would be hers. Today Valentine cards are often left unsigned so that the receiver cannot be sure who her Valentine is.

*February 14th*
**Blessing the Nets**
**Northam-on-Tweed, Northumberland**
This old ceremony of the blessing of the nets is carried out at midnight between the February 14th and 15th at Pedwell. There is a short service when the fishermen, the boats and the nets are blessed, all carefully organized so that the first boat of the season sets out immediately after midnight. If the first shot of net contains a salmon, it is handed to the Vicar.

This custom takes place on Monday, February 15th or 16th if either the 14th or 15th is a Sunday.

*February 14th*
**King's Lynn Fair**
**King's Lynn, Norfolk**
This six-day charter fair dates back to the 11th century.

It is opened by the Mayor who has the first go on the roundabout.

*February: moveable*
**Sri Ramakrishna's Birthday**
Sri Ramakrishna, a Hindu saint who lived in the 19th century, started the Ramakrishna Vedanta movement.

*February 20th (or near)*
**Sir John Cass Service**
**London: St Botolph's, Aldgate**
Sir John Cass, who was born in 1661 and died in 1718, was a wealthy man who was concerned with the education of poor children. He decided to found a school but just as he was about to sign his will leaving the bequest, he had a very bad haemorrhage. Although he was dying, he managed to scrawl his name, but his quill pen became covered in his blood. Every year, on the anniversary of his death, pupils, staff and governors of the school and college named after him go to his commemoration service, the girls wearing red quills in their berets in memory of him.

**Shrovetide**
*February: moveable*
Shrovetide usually falls in February, but occasionally it occurs early in March. As you know, it comes immediately before the beginning of Lent which starts on Ash Wednesday, the day after Shrove Tuesday, and goes on until Good Friday. Lent is the time when Christians try to live more simply, some people giving up things they really enjoy.

Lent used to be taken very seriously. Housewives did their best to use up food that was not going to be eaten during that period — foods like eggs, butter and fat — and so one of the dishes they made was pancakes. Shrove Tuesday or Fastern E'en was known as Bannock Tuesday in Scotland since the Scots made thick flat cakes made of oatmeal or barley meal which were cooked on a griddle.

Lent was also a time for quiet and meditation, and so on Shrove Tuesday people let off steam by taking part in games and competitions, and that explains why so many games of Shrovetide Football are played in various parts of the country.

*Shrove Tuesday*
**Shrovetide Football**
**Alnwick, Northumberland**
At one time this game was played in the streets, but these days the pitch is a field with the goals decorated with greenery and standing about a quarter of a mile apart. Like most of these games, any number can play, and often well over a hundred crowd onto the pitch.

The ball is kept in Alnwick Castle. Off goes a committee to fetch it, and they return with the Duke of Northumberland's piper who plays his bagpipes as the ball is carried onto the pitch.

The teams, those from the parishes of St Paul's and St Michael's, play only with their feet, unlike many other games, and they don't stop until there have been three goals, each announced by the sounding of a trumpet. It all finishes with a mad scramble to get the ball off the pitch.

*Shrove Tuesday*
**Shrovetide Football**
**Corfe Castle, Dorset**
The quarries at Purbeck used to be very important. In fact, St Paul's Cathedral in London is built of Purbeck marble. The quarrymen have a right of way to what used to be the chief harbour, so to maintain their rights, just in case they want to use it in the future, they punt a football along the old road to Ower Quay.

The game follows the meeting of the Court of the Company of Marblers, and it is then that new apprentices are admitted to the craft.

*Shrove Tuesday and Ash Wednesday*
**Shrovetide Football**
**Ashbourne, Derbyshire**
As if one wild game of football isn't enough, the people of Ashbourne play it on two succeeding days. The footballs are quite different from any others. They are made of leather and are stuffed with cork dust, and then painted white and often decorated with the Union Jack.

Here the teams are known as Up'ards and Down'ards, depending on whether the players come from the north or south of the River Henmore. The goals are the mills at Clifton and Sturston, nearly 5 kilometres (3 miles) apart, and a lot of heaving and shoving goes on round and in the River Henmore and other streams that wind across the pitch. The game starts at 2 pm and goes on for hours. Then, wet, dirty, and exhausted, everyone goes home and prepares for the next day's battle.

*Shrove Tuesday*
**Shrovetide Football**
**Atherstone, Warwickshire**
There's an important difference in this game of football, for women and children can take part if they feel strong enough. The football is filled with water so that it doesn't travel very far, and it starts life decorated with red, white and blue ribbons. Once upon a time the teams were either men from Warwickshire or Leicestershire, and it is thought that this game originated in the reign of King John. Now it's an every-man-for-himself game.

It begins promptly at 2 pm and lasts for three hours, the ball being contested for up and down the main road. At the end of the game whoever has the ball keeps it.

*Shrove Tuesday*
**Shrovetide Football**
**Sedgefield, Co Durham**
If you are in Sedgefield and want to join in, listen for the Pancake Bell. It rings at about midday to remind you that the game is going to start at 1 pm. Although the ball is small, the pitch is a tough one in a sense. The goals are about half a mile apart, but they are both ponds. You'd think that goalies would wear mackintoshes and wellies, wouldn't you?

*Shrove Tuesday*
**Shrovetide Football**
**St Columb Major, St Columb Minor, Cornwall**
This is a game of Cornish hurling, and again it is played with a small light ball which must be tossed and not kicked, but vigorous rugby-like tackles are allowed. The game starts at about 4 pm and is played between the Townsmen and

the Countrymen, and each team might have hundreds of players. On the ball is written:
> *Town and country, do your best,*
> *For in this parish I must rest.*

*Shrove Tuesday*
**Pancake Day Race**
**Olney, Buckinghamshire**
This old traditional race in Olney goes back at least 500 years. The story is that a housewife was busy making pancakes when she heard the church bell calling her to a service. Startled, and not wanting to be late, off she rushed to church, still wearing her apron and still clutching her frying pan.

This developed into the famous race. It is for women only, and each must wear a head-covering and an apron. The Pancake Bell is run at 11.30 am and then again at 11.45. The competitors line up, pancakes in pans, and exactly at 11.55 the race begins. As the women and girls rush over the course of about 366 metres (400 yards), they have to toss their pancakes three times as they go. The winner gets a kiss, and she and the runner-up each receive a prayer book.

Since 1950 there has been friendly rivalry between the people of Liberal, Kansas, USA where a similar race is run over a course the same length. Liberal rings up Olney to find out the winner's time and to compare results.

*Shrove Tuesday*
**Pancake Greaze**
**London: Westminster School**
At 11 am a verger from Westminster Abbey leads a procession into the school, and he is followed by the cook, dressed in sparkling white and carrying a large frying pan containing a large pancake. He tosses this over a 4.8 metre (16 foot) high iron bar which separates the Upper and Lower Schools, and the boys scramble for it. The boy who manages to get out of this wild scrum with the largest piece of pancake wins a cash prize, and so does the cook.

*Shrove Tuesday*
**Skipping**
**Scarborough, North Yorkshire**
Skipping used to be a fairly common Shrovetide custom at the beginning of this century, but in most places it has died out. In Scarborough the Pancake Bell is rung at around noon and at about 2 pm men, women and children make their way down to the foreshore to skip.

*Shrove Tuesday*
**Egg-Shackling**
**Stoke St Gregory, Somerset**
Children take eggs to school and write their names on them, and then they are carefully placed in a sieve. Then the eggs are shaken very gently — this is the shackling. Once an egg has cracked it is removed from the sieve and this continues until only one unbroken egg is left. Sometimes a prize is given to the person whose egg is left.

*Ash Wednesday*
**Worshipful Company of Stationers' Service**
**London: St Paul's Cathedral**
This ceremony takes place on Ash Wednesday, the Wednesday that comes immediately after Shrove Tuesday. John Norton, a member of this Company, left a sum of money to pay for a service to be held in St Faith's Chapel in Old St Paul's. The cathedral was burned in the Great Fire of London in 1666, but the service still goes on. Now you will see a splendid procession of members dressed in their

furred gowns and velvet caps going to St Paul's from Stationers' Hall and back again. Once they've disappeared inside they tuck into cakes and ale.

# March

*March 1st*
**St David's Day**
St David, the patron saint of Wales, was traditionally a prince who was the uncle of King Arthur. He was a very holy man who founded an abbey at Menevia. Since he was supposed to have lived for years on nothing but bread and wild leeks perhaps that is why the leek became a Welsh emblem, although the official one is the daffodil. There are ceremonial distributions of leeks to soldiers in Welsh regiments on this day.

*March 1st*
**Whuppity Scoorie**
**Lanark, Strathclyde**
The origin of this custom is not really known. Some think it is meant to welcome the spring, others that it is to scare away evil spirits, and the more bloodthirsty that it commemorates the escape of an English soldier from Wallace and his men. He rushed to the church for sanctuary and just managed to get inside to safety. Whatever the reason, it's popular with the Lanark children.

For some reason the town bell is silent between October and February but at 6 pm you'll see the young people standing by the church, waiting for the bell to ring for the first time in months. As the bell begins to ring, the children, all armed with balls of tightly wrapped paper on the end of a string, race three times round the church, whirling their weapons and whacking others with them, trying to be first. There's a prize for the winner and a scramble for pennies by the rest.

*March: moveable*
### Ram Navmi
Hindus celebrate the birthday of Lord Rama on this day with prayers. He is the central figure in a Sanskrit epic poem, the Ramayanam, which tells of his adventure. Rama is often identified with Vishnu, the preserver.

*March: second Tuesday*
### Thanksgiving
### Royal Hospital, Bridewell
This is a service of dedication and thanksgiving for the foundation of the Royal Hospital, Bridewell. Be there at about midday if you want to see the Lord Mayor, the Sheriffs, and pupils of King Edward VI School at Whitley as they process into the church.

*March: Sunday in the middle of the month*
### Grimaldi Commemoration Service
### London: Holy Trinity Church, Dalston
This is a must for those who are keen on the circus, and on clowns in particular. Joseph Grimaldi, who was born in 1779 and died in 1837, was a much-loved man and a brilliant clown who actually invented the clown's dress. In fact, clowns are called 'Joey' after him.

If you turn up at church, you'll see an amazing sight. Clowns in full regalia with painted faces, false noses, and sometimes with large feet and carrying balloons crowd in the church for a simple but happy commemoration service. They sing the memorial hymn, *Lord of the Dance*, and are presented with posies of spring flowers collected by children in Devon.

*March 17th*
### St Patrick's Day
St Patrick is the patron saint of Ireland. He was actually born in Britain, but was carried off to Ireland by pirates. There he worked as a swineherd for six years before he managed to escape. Then he went off and trained as a priest before returning to Ireland. It is commonly believed that snakes wriggle away if they come into contact with shamrock and since St Patrick used it to explain the

meaning of the Trinity, he is believed to have rid the country of snakes. Thousands of people visit Downpatrick, the place where tradition says he was buried, and Saul, where he founded the first church in Ireland, on this day.

## *March: third Thursday*
## Kipling Cotes Derby
## South Dalton, Humberside

This is the oldest horse race in the world, and it has been run for over 450 years. In fact, once when there were no competitors, the organizers walked a horse round the course rather than break the tradition. The course covers five parishes and starts at South Dalton and finishes near Kipling Cotes Farm. The competitors pay a fee to enter the race, they have to weigh at least 63 kilograms (10 stones), and they have to mind their manners since the rules say that 'no rider that layeth hold on, or striketh another rider shall receive any prize whatsoever.'

The race starts promptly at noon, everyone gallops off, and the winner receives the interest on the money left to endow the race. The person who comes second does rather better — he gets all of the stake money.

## *March 25th*
## Tichborne Dole
## Tichborne, Hampshire

In the 12th century, when the kind Lady Mabella, the wife of the harsh Sir Roger de Tichborne, lay dying, she begged her husband to provide a dole for the poor. He must have had a warped sense of humour, for he grabbed a burning faggot from the fire and said he would give as much land for the dole as she could cover before the flame went out.

Although she was desperately ill, Lady Mabella insisted on being carried outside. She held the burning brand and, although her strength was fast ebbing, managed to crawl round the 9 hectares (23 acres) of land still known as the Crawls before the flame flickered and died. Exhausted though she was, she warned her husband that unless the dole was kept up, there would be a generation of seven sons and then one of seven daughters, that the house would fall down, and that the family would die out.

Alarmed, Sir Roger kept his word, and so did his descendants until in the 19th century, Sir Henry Tichborne gave money to the church instead of the dole. Oddly enough, there was a generation of seven sons and then a generation of seven daughters, and part of the house did fall down. The dole was quickly restored, and so, right up to today, the people of Tichborne, Cheriton and Lane End receive a dole of flour which has come from wheat grown on the Crawls.

*March 31st (or as near as possible)*
**Oranges and Lemons Service**
**London: St Clement Danes Church**
This is a special church service for the children of St Clement Danes Primary School in Drury Lane. Off they go to the church for a short service which starts at 3 pm, the famous nursery rhyme tune is played on handbells, and an orange and a lemon is given to each child. The tune is also played on the church bells four times a day.

**Holy Week**

*March or April: moveable*
**Maundy Thursday**
**Maundy Money Service**
**Westminster Abbey, London, or some other cathedral**
Christ washed the feet of his disciples the day before he was crucified. It became the custom for the rich and powerful to do the same. The monarch used to follow this custom, but it died out during the reign of James II. However, there is still a very important ceremony. The Queen distributes specially minted money to poor people. The amount given depends upon the Queen's age — there is one penny for each of her years.

There is a magnificent procession into the cathedral, and a service. Then the distribution of the Maundy money takes place. A Yeoman of the Guard holds a huge tray containing white and red leather purses, and the Queen passes down the line of poor people presenting them with the purses. The Maundy money is in the white purses. The red ones also have money. This is to make up for the fact that clothes and food are no longer given as they used to be.

You will see that the Queen is carrying a small bouquet of flowers and sweet herbs. This is to protect her from the plague — not that there's likely to be one today, but there used to be violent outbreaks right into the early 18th century. The clergy have linen towels on their shoulders. That's to remind everyone of the ritual foot-washing.

*Good Friday*
**Hot Cross Buns**
This is the day when Jesus was crucified, and Christians go to special services in church to remember the sacrifice he made.

It seems curious that this is the day when we eat hot cross buns. Like so many other customs, this goes a long way back in history, ages before the coming of Christianity. Greeks and Romans used to eat small cakes early in spring, and it is thought that Saxons did so too. However, they were changed into Christian symbols instead of pagan ones, by the addition of the cross which is to remind people of the way that Christ died.

Most people buy hot cross buns from the baker, but at one time they were either made by hardworking housewives early on Good Friday morning, or later on, they were bought from a baker who carried them around the streets in a tray covered with a white cloth. As he strolled along he shouted 'Hot Cross Buns! Hot Cross Buns! One a penny, two a penny, Hot Cross Buns!'

According to tradition, a bun made on Good Friday morning will never go bad or mouldy if it is made properly and stored in a dry place. These buns were kept as a kind of medicine since they were thought to cure a whole string of illnesses including whooping-cough and dysentery, and even in the 19th century it was not unusual to see them strung from the kitchen ceiling.

*Good Friday*
**Orange Rolling**
**Dunstable Downs, Bedfordshire**
Hundreds of children gather on the downs to roll oranges down Pascombe Pit. This is believed to be symbolic of the rolling away of the stone from the entrance of Jesus' tomb.

*Good Friday*
**Marbles Championship**
**Tinsley Green, West Sussex**
In 1600, so the story goes, two men wanted to marry the same girl. Their rivalry became greater and greater, and finally they decided they would have to settle the matter with a fight, but intead of using swords or pistols, they chose to have a marbles contest. What the girl thought or whether she even fancied one of them isn't known.

The result of all this is that Tinsley holds the World Marble Championship, but instead of the winner receiving a girl, he gets a silver cup.

There is a large concrete ring sprinkled with sand, and each member of each team tries to knock out as many marbles as possible from the ring. Finally, the winner of the year's competition plays the winner of the previous year. It is hoped that there will a junior marbles championship in the future.

*Good Friday*
**Pace-Egg Play**
**Midgeley, Sowerby Bridge, West Yorkshire**
The boys of Calder High School, wearing helmet-type hats and brightly coloured tunics decorated with ribbons and rosettes, perform a mummer's play. St George, the hero, fights Bold Slasher, Bold Hector, and the Black Prince of Paradine. You can tell St George is the goodie since a bugler always announces his arrival. There are other characters — a Doctor, the King of Egypt, a Fool, and Tosspot, a devilish character with a straw tail. He carries a straw basket for contributions. At one time people put eggs into the basket to show their appreciation of the mummers, but nowadays they toss in coins.

*Good Friday*
**Butterworth Charity**
**London: St Bartholomew the Great**
Twenty-one poor widows over the age of sixty each receive sixpence after a service in the church. The money is placed on a tombstone in the churchyard together with twenty-one hot cross buns. Each widow kneels by the stone, picks up

her sixpence, crosses the stone and is given the bun and another small sum of money.

This is an old dole, but like so many charities, the funds began to run out. After all, what looked like a lot of money several hundreds of years ago is worth very little today. However, in the 19th century a man called Joshua Butterwoth re-endowed the charity rather than see the custom die out. Since the name of the original donor was forgotten, the charity has been known by Butterworth's name ever since.

*Good Friday*
**Barrington Dole**
**Ideford, Devon**
In 1585 Bartholomew Barrington left land so that twenty new shillings could be laid on his tomb and presented to twenty poor people. This used to take place on Maundy Thursday but now the Rector and the Churchwardens make the presentation on the following day.

*Good Friday*
**Burning of Judas**
**Liverpool, Merseyside**
A few children keep up this old custom. In the south end of Liverpool near the docks you might see small bands of children carrying straw-stuffed effigies going from house to house. The effigies are raised on poles and banged on upper windows with a shout of 'Judas is short of a penny for his breakfast!' No doubt kind-hearted householders see that he doesn't go hungry. Later there are bonfires and a lot of Judases go up in flames.

**Easter**

Easter marks the end of Lent. It is always on the Sunday following the first full moon appearing on or after March 21st. It's all a bit confusing, but it does explain why people talk about Easter coming early or late. In fact the earliest possible date for Easter is March 21st and the latest is April 25th.

This is both a sad and a happy Christian festival since it

commemorates the events that led up to the crucifixion of Christ and his resurrection three days later. Eggs are symbols of a new life, so this is why we give each other Easter eggs.

*Easter Saturday*
**Britannia Coconut Dancers**
**Bacup, Lancashire**
The Britannia Coconut Dancers need to be very fit for they perform from one side of the town to the other, a distance of about 11 kilometres (7 miles).

There are members of the team and a whipper-in who goes in front of them to drive away evil spirits. Their dress is quite different from any other dancers. They have red and white skirts worn over black breeches, white stockings and black clogs, and their faces are blackened. In their hands they hold wooden discs. These 'nuts' are actually made from the tops of bobbins, and as they dance they clap them against other nuts attached to their knees. The music is usually provided by a band, but at one time it was traditionally provided by a concertina player.

*Easter Monday*
**Biddenden Dole**
**Biddenden, Kent**
If you happen to be in Biddenden at 10 am you might well be given a Biddenden cake. Actually it's more like a hard biscuit. If you look at it you will see that it has on it the figures of two women very close to each other. The names of the two sisters are above the figures and the name of the village underneath. On the apron of one of the figures the number '34' is stamped, and on the other is 'in 1100'.

This all refers to Siamese twins. Tradition says that they were born in 1100, although most people think that they were born much later. Anyway, they were joined together by ligaments at the shoulders and hips. One of them died at the age of thirty-four. Friends begged her sister to have the ligaments cut so that she could live. She refused, saying that as they had come into the world together, so they should go out together, and a few hours later she too died.

The land left to endow this charity was called Bread and Cheese Land because the villagers received a dole of bread and cheese from the rent of the land. The dole is now distributed from the window of a cottage that stands on the land.

*Easter Monday*
**Hare-Pie Scramble and Bottle Kicking**
**Hallaton, Leicestershire**
Many years ago a piece of land was left to the rector of the parish but in return he had to provide two hare pies, two dozen loaves to be scrambled for, as well as some ale.

The pies, now no longer made from hare, are taken to the church and blessed, and then they are taken to Hare-Pie Bank where they are cut up and scrambled for.

Later on everyone assembles and a band leads a procession up to the Bank for the bottle-kicking. Actually there aren't any bottles. There are three small wooden kegs, one empty and two filled with beer. The teams get ready for the struggle. The men of Hallaton eye the men from Medbourne, and the Medbourne men look over their rivals. A filled bottle is tossed in the air and the tussle starts. The object of the match is to get the bottle over the opposing team's goal — these are two streams about a mile apart. Once this bottle has been won, the empty one is fought for, and finally the last full one. Then off they all go to the Cross where the beer is drunk. By that time they must need it.

*Easter Monday*
**Coal Carrying Championship**
**Ossett, West Yorkshire**
You really need some muscles to enter this championship. Starting at 12.30 pm men carry 50 kilograms (a hundredweight) of coal over a hard uphill course of nearly a mile. The start is from the Royal Oak, Ossett, and the finish at The Maypole, Gawthorpe. The winner receives cash, a trophy, a gold medal and, perhaps most welcome of all, a keg of beer.

This is followed by a women's race. Their course is 91 metres (100 yards) long and they each carry 12.5 kilograms (28 pounds) of solid fuel. I suppose it's reasonable enough that since the course is shorter and the load lighter, the prize is smaller.

*Easter Monday*
**Pace-Egging**
**Preston, Lancashire**
Swarms of children collect in Avenham Park to roll their brightly coloured eggs down steep slopes. Like the orange rolling at Dunstable, this is symbolic of the rolling aside of the stone sealing Christ's tomb.

*Easter Monday*
**Running Auction**
**Bourne, Lincolnshire**
White Bread Meadow was left by Richard Clayton in 1770 to provide for a dole of bread to the poor. The rent from the land provided the money for the bread, but this land had to be auctioned.

Two boys run up and down a stretch of road. If someone makes a bid while they are running, then that bid wins, but if another is made while they are still on the trot, they have to start again. The auction only ends when no second bid has been made. The boys get a reward, and everyone goes off for a bread, cheese and beer supper.

*Hocktide Tuesday*
**Hocktide Tutti-men**
**Hungerford, Berkshire**
What is Hocktide? Well, the Sunday following Easter Sunday is called Low Sunday. Hocktide is the Monday and Tuesday after Low Sunday. Rents used to be paid at this time of the year, and people used to collect money for the church. It was also a great time for sports and games, but this custom has died out almost everywhere.

It hasn't in Hungerford where Hocktide Tuesday (remember, this is the second Tuesday after Easter) is a very important day. This town doesn't have a Mayor and Corporation. Instead there is a governing body of men called Feoffees, a High Constable, a Portreeve, Tutti-men and other officials. These men are elected on Hocktide Tuesday at 9 am.

At 8 am the Town Crier stands on the Town Hall balcony and blows his bugle-horn. The Bellman, smartly dressed in grey and scarlet and wearing a tall hat, rings his bell telling everyone to go to the Court House for the election.

While the Court is sitting, off go the Tutti-men and the Orange Scrambler. The Tutti-men each have tall poles which are decorated with spring flowers and ribbons, and stuck on top of the pole is an orange. The Orange Scrambler carries a sack of oranges. Their job is to visit every commoner's house in the town — about a hundred of them — to collect their dues, the princely sum of one penny. However, they are prepared to accept a kiss from women and girls instead. In return they hand up the orange on the spiked pole and the Orange Scrambler replaces it with another. Any oranges left over are scrambled for by children.

At the end of their rounds they go back to the Three Swans for a civic lunch. A special punch is brewed and then another odd ceremony takes place. If any of the guests are strangers to Hungerford, the Constable points it out and announces that the colt must be shod. In comes a blacksmith and another man who is carrying nails. The visitor is held and a pretence is made of driving nails into the soles of his shoes. It only stops when he shouts 'Punch!' and pays for another round of drinks.

The following Friday the new officials are sworn in. There is a dinner in the evening and the health of John of Gaunt is drunk, for it was this nobleman who, hundreds of years ago, gave the townspeople special privileges including free fishing rights in the River Kennet.

# April

*April 5th (or near)*
**John Stow Commemoration Service**
**London: St Andrew Undershaft Church**
John Stow, who wrote the *Survey of London* in 1598, is remembered on the anniversary of his death. An effigy of him in the church shows him busily writing with a quill pen fixed between his fingers. At the service an address is given by a noted historian and the Lord Mayor removes the old quill pen and replaces it with a new one. A prize is given to the schoolchild who has written the best essay on

London in an annual competition, and the school the prize-winner has come from is given the old quill pen. This service is usually held at midday.

*April: moveable*
## Ching Ming
The Chinese are marvellous to old people, and they are also very conscientious about the dead. For three days before this occasion they don't light fires or eat hot food. Then, on this day, off they go to the graves of their ancestors, plant flowers and generally tidy them up. They also offer imitation clothes, money and furniture — in fact, anything that they might have used during their lifetime. Later these offerings are ceremoniously burned.

*April 6th (Tuesday following)*
## Stowell Court Auction
**Tatworth, Somerset**
The Stowell Court meets to auction land known as Stowell Mead. A tallow candle is lit, and as long as it is burning, bids are accepted. The person who makes the last bid before the flame goes out is the winner and has the use of the land for the next twelve months. It's worth putting in a bid since there's a supper of bread, cheese and watercress afterwards for all those who have taken part in the auction.

*April: moveable*
## Passover
Passover recalls the time when the Jewish people escaped from slavery in Egypt. Although Pharaoh promised to let them go, he did not, even though various plagues were inflicted on the Egyptian people. Finally, the eldest son in every family was killed, but the Jewish children escaped because the doors of their houses had been smeared with the blood of a lamb, and so the Angel of Death passed over them.

During the period of this festival, Jews do not eat leavened bread, but they do have a commemorative meal in their houses. There are special foods, all of which have a meaning — there is the shank bone of lamb, a roasted egg, bitter herbs, a mixture of apples and nuts, watercress, unleavened bread and wine. At this meal the youngest child asks the father four questions, and the answers to the questions actually tell the story of the escape from Egypt.

*April: moveable*
**Baisakhi**
In 1699 Guru Gobind Singh (*see* p 7) baptised his first five disciples. This ceremony, known as Amrit, is the time when people can be baptised into the Sikh faith.

*April 19th*
**Primrose Day Ceremony**
**London: Parliament Square**
This is the anniversary of the death in 1881 of Benjamin Disraeli, a famous Tory statesman and really the founder of the modern Conservative party. Members of the Primrose Society meet and lay these lovely spring flowers at the foot of his statue.

*April 23rd*
**St George's Day**
St George is the patron saint of England, but just who he was and how he became the patron saint is not too clear. It is thought that he was martyred at Lydda in Palestine, and that his cult was actually brought to this country by the Crusaders. Whatever the reason, his feast day became very popular, and this increased when Edward III founded the Order of the Garter under the patronage of the saint. You'll see that some people remember his day by wearing roses in their buttonholes. It seems a pity, but somehow he doesn't seem very likely to have killed a dragon.

*April 23rd*
**Shakespeare's Birthday Celebrations**
**Stratford-upon-Avon, Warwickshire**
This is a truly international celebration since representatives from dozens of countries are invited, all of them walking in an impressive procession carrying wreaths of flowers to be placed on his tomb, while the flags of all the nations taking part are unfurled. Festivities including dancing and singing start in mid-morning and go on right through to the evening when there is a special birthday performance at the theatre.

*April: last Sunday*
**Tyburn Walk**
**London: Old Bailey-Marble Arch**
This walk which starts promptly at 3 pm is in memory of those Catholic martyrs who died for their faith in the 16th and 17th centuries. The walk which passes Ely Place, Kingsway, Soho Square and Oxford Street follows as far as possible the route along which the victims were taken from Newgate prison to the Tyburn gallows.

# May

**May Day**
Until the Puritans came to power after the Civil Wars, May Day was not only an important festival, but it was also a very gay one. It actually originated in the old Roman festival of Flora, the goddess of fruit and flowers.

People used to get up very early in the morning to go a-Maying. Nowhere was very far from the country in those days and so even those who lived in cities and towns joined in, and they all came back bearing flowers and greenery which were used to decorate houses, public buildings and, most importantly, the Maypole. Many girls bathed their faces in May dew so that their skins would be beautiful throughout the year.

Some towns and villages still have maypoles and elect a May Queen, but at one time there was a Lord of the May as well. Jack-in-the Green was a kind of jester who capered around underneath a large frame which was completely covered in greenery.

This is the day when many groups of Morris dancers take to the streets and you'll see them, gaily dressed, sometimes tinkling with bells, sometimes whacking sticks together or twirling handkerchiefs as they dance, while in northern England in particular, you might see them dancing with swords.

May Day is now an official holiday again, but it is not always going to occur on May 1st. This makes it difficult to write about festivities since some will take place on May Day itself, some on the official holiday, and others on the nearest Saturday. If you want to see something in particular you'll have to get in touch with the nearest Tourist Board Information Centre or write to the Town Hall.

*May 1st (also 19 September)*
**Garland Dressing**
**Charlton-on-Otmoor, Oxfordshire**
If you go in the village church you'll see the Garland by the rood screen. This large cross is covered in clipped yew. Twice a year it is taken down and redressed. On May Day children take little flower-covered crosses to the service, and these are later carried round the village. This probably stems from the days when statues from the church were taken in procession round the streets. This is a place where there is a May Queen and May Day dances.

*May 1st*
**Hobby-Horse**
**Minehead, Somerset**
Minehead's Hobby-Horse is a fierce creature. His long frame is carried on a man's shoulders, and they are both covered by a tough cloth decorated with circles. The horse's head in the centre of the frame has a twisted collection of coloured ribbons, and he has a long tail to swish around.

Swaying to the music as he ambles around, he first appears on the evening before May Day, lashing his tail wildly at those who ignore his collecting box. He reappears on May Day and prances off with his attendants to Dunster Castle, Dunster, and then back home again.

*May 1st*
**Hobby-Horse**
**Padstow, Cornwall**
''Obby 'Oss' or 'Old 'Oss,' as Padstow's Hobby-horse is known, consists of a hoop-shaped frame covered with a black tarpaulin which a man climbs into. His head is hidden by a ferocious mask with a tall, pointed hat perched on top.

The wooden head has snapper-jaws and he had, naturally, a tail as well. He is always accompanied by the Teaser who wears odd clothes and carries a sort of padded club.

The celebrations begin late on the evening before May Day when the Mayers go round Padstow singing the lovely Night Song. Sometimes they stand outside people's houses and greet them by name in the song. Then, in the morning, out prances Old 'Oss from the yard of the Golden Lion, and off he sets, dancing and capering about, chasing girls and trying to cover them in his tarpaulin skirt. Every now and again he dies a magical death. As he sinks down the jaunty Night Song dies away and the slower, sadder Day Song is heard. Teaser strokes him gently with his club, and then the Night Song is heard. Up leaps Old 'Oss, gambolling around, alive once more.

Padstow has a second Hobby-Horse, Temperance, or Blue Ribbon. Once he was a rival, but now he dances round a different part of the town and only meets Old 'Oss by the Maypole in the market square.

*May 1st*
**May Morning Ceremony**
**Oxford, Oxfordshire**
At 6 am the choristers of Magdelen College go to the top of the tower to greet the sunrise with traditional carols, while down below hundreds listen. After the singing and the pealing of bells, the Oxford and Headington Morris Dancers perform throughout the city.

*May 1st*
**Riding of the Bounds**
**Berwick-on-Tweed, Northumberland**
Early in the morning riders converge on Berwick on Tweed to take part in the ceremonial riding of the boundaries. The Mayor does it in the easy way — riding in a coach — and all complete the 16 kilometre (10 mile) circuit finishing at 2.15 pm.

*May: first Saturday*
**Gawthorpe Feast**
**Gawthorpe, Ossett, West Yorkshire**
Go and see the Maypole procession which goes from

Gawthorpe village to Ossett market place. The May Queen and her six maids of honour lead the way, all on horseback and preceded by a band, with up to 100 other riders, decorated floats, bands, dancers and lots of people in fancy dress. This magnificent procession returns to the village in the late afternoon when the May Queen is crowned and prizes for the best entries in the procession distributed. If the weather is good enough there is Maypole dancing. The day finishes with a traditional fair.

*May 2nd (First Wednesday following)*
**St Ethelbert's Fair**
**Hereford, Hereford and Worcester**
This fair has been taking place for centuries. Once it was always held on May 19th and lasted for nine days. The Bishop used to receive the tolls, and the longer it lasted, the better he did out of it. Then it was reduced to two days, and so were the Bishop's takings. Now, although this has become a pleasure fair, some wheat is handed over to the Bishop's agent. But this, of course, is only a token of the Bishop's right to receive the tolls. *See* Charter Fairs p 90.

*May 8th*
**Furry Dance**
**Helston, Cornwall**
This is a really happy occasion. All the houses and buildings are decorated with flowers and greenery. The church bells ring, there is a service, and then the Early Morning Dance begins. Off the dancers go, along the streets, round squares, and in and out of gardens. Others collect even more flowers and greenery, and accompanied by St George, Robin Hood, and other folk characters, they stand singing at fixed points.

At about 10 am, the spectacular Children's Dance begins, with up to 1000 children taking part. At midday the Principal Dance begins from the Guildhall. Led by the Mayor, the couples set off, the men wearing morning-coats, the women in summer frocks, all of them wearing lilies-of-the-valley. Round the town they go, in and out of shops and houses, preferably going in by one door and out by another, since that's the luckiest way to do it.

At 5 pm there's a final dance, this time led by young

people, and at last the spectators who must have been getting itchy feet watching all that dancing, are allowed to join in. The Helston Town Band must be pretty exhausted by the end of the day. It is estimated that they play their way over 24 kilometres (15 miles) during the day.

*May 9th*
**Stow-on-the-Wold Fair**
**Stow-on-the-Wold, Gloucestershire**
This fair, founded by Edward IV in 1476, started off by being a sheep fair. However, as sheep became less important to the economy of the town, it became a horse fair. *See* Charter Fairs p 90.

*May 13th*
**Garland Day**
**Abbotsbury, Dorset**
May 13th used to be old May Day (*see* The Old Calendar p 93) so perhaps that is the reason why this village celebrates Garland Day on that date. Originally Abbotsbury had a small fishing fleet and so, to mark the beginning of the fishing season, garlands were made, carried to the church for a service, and then taken to the boats and later thrown overboard with a prayer or a hymn.

Then the custom changed. Children carried the huge garlands round the streets and placed them on the War Memorial. In 1975 it was decided that one of the garlands should be thrown into the sea, and so the old custom has been revived.

*May 14th (nearest Wednesday)*
**Beating the Bounds**
**Newbiggin-by-the-Sea, Northumberland**
Freeholders of Newbiggin ride the bounds (*see* Beating the Bounds p 90) each year to keep their rights to the moor.

*May: second or third week*
**Spring Flower Parade**
**Spalding, Lincolnshire**
It was only in 1958 that Spalding decided to have a spring flower parade, but it is already an enormous attraction. Dozens of floats decorated with millions of tulip heads

leave the Sir Halley Stewart Field at 1.30 pm and go on a 7 kilometres (4.5 mile) journey through the streets of Spalding to the Springfield Arena and back again. All roads are closed during this parade and visitors must arrive before noon. The floats are on show at the Sir Halley Stewart Field on the parade day and for the following three days.

During this period there are stunning displays of flowers in the churches of the town and in the surrounding villages. Get in touch with the East Midlands Tourist Board for further information.

*May: third Wednesday*
**Mayoring Day**
**Sandwich, Kent**
Preparations for this ceremony begin in the previous October when the Town Sergeant goes off and cuts a blackthorn stick. Over a period of time it is straightened and then lacquered. This is presented to the Mayor as his wand of office. Lucky fellow — witches will steer clear of him for the rest of the year.

*May 20th*
**Weighing the Mayor**
**High Wycombe, Buckinghamshire**
The Mayor and other officials are weighed in public in an ancient ceremony here, and so is the ex-Mayor. The Beadle rings his bell and after the traditional, 'Oyez, Oyez, Oyez,' he shouts out the weight and any variation in it from the previous year.

It is thought that this curious custom is to show the citizens just how industrious the officials have been. Those who worked hard probably lost weight, and those who took it easy probably gained weight. Probably some slimming goes on just before the weighing in!

*May 21st*
**Lilies and Roses Ceremony**
**London: Tower of London**
This commemorates the murder of Henry VI in the Wakefield Tower in 1471. Because this king founded both King's College, Cambridge, and Eton College, representatives

from these educational establishments join a procession in the Tower of London and lay roses and lilies on the spot where he was killed.

*May 25th*
**Maypole Dancing**
**Ickwell, Bedfordshire**
There's a spectacular maypole on Ickwell village green. It's about 23 metres (70 feet) high and is painted in spirals. As children dance round it, two Moggies with blackened faces and wearing curious clothes and carrying besom brooms prance around with a collecting box. Whether they pretend to whack you with the brooms depends on what you give.

*May: last Wednesday*
**Samuel Pepys' Day**
**London: St Olave's Church**
This service, which usually begins at 12 am, is to commemorate Samuel Pepys, the famous diarist. It is attended by members of the Pepys' Club, representatives of the Admiralty, Trinity House, the Royal Society and others. The music played is from the 17th century, there is an address, and a laurel wreath is placed on the Pepys' memorial.

*May: last Monday*
**Common Walk**
**Laugharne, Dyfed**
This takes quite a lot of stamina — the distance covered is over 32 kilometres (20 miles) so it needs an early start. At 5 am the Bailiff rings a bell. The Portreeve arrives and so do the halbardmen, the Common Attorney, and the Grand Jury, and off they go, stopping now and then to beat the bounds (*see* page 90) and, not unnaturally, to have something to eat or drink. This event takes place every three years, so the officials have time to get into training. The next Common Walk will take place in 1981.

*May 29th*
**Dressing the Arbor Tree**
**Aston-on-Clun, Shropshire**
In 1786 John Marston married Mary Carter, and a black

poplar was decorated with flags for the occasion. It seems that the bride was so pleased when she saw the decorations that she left a sum of money so that it could be repeated each year.

Some people think that it marks an older custom when a tree was decorated with flags to keep the witches away.

*May 29th*
### 1346 Commemoration Service
### Durham Cathedral, Durham
This commemorates the defeat of the Scots in 1346. The English and Scots were lined up for battle, and it seemed likely that the Scots would win. The night before the battle the Prior had a vivid dream, and when he awoke he carried out the dream. Picking up a cloth, a relic of St Cuthbert, he made his way to a hilltop near the battlefield and held it out like a banner. As the day wore on it became clear that the Scots were defeated. Meanwhile, the monks were assembled on the top of the tower watching eagerly. They chanted masses for the English army and as soon as they knew of its victory, they sang a Te Deum.

In memory of this occasion, the Cathedral choir mounts the tower and sing anthems facing north, south and east in turn.

*May 29th*
### Grovely Forest Rights
### Wishford Magna, Wiltshire
The people who live here are woken up early in the morning with shouts of 'Grovely, Grovely, and all Grovely!' Up they get and off they go to the woods where they cut green boughs, bring them back, and set them up in front of the houses in the village. A procession forms up and marches through the streets behind a banner which proclaims 'Grovely! Grovely! Grovely! And all Grovely! Unity is strength!' Four women carrying bundles of faggots on their heads follow. With others, they then go to Salisbury Cathedral where oak sprigs are laid on the altar.

On their return to the village they are met by a procession of villagers, most of them wearing fancy-dress. Accompanied by a band, the parade winds its way round the streets again and then everyone settles down for a well-deserved ceremonial lunch. This is followed by traditional games and entertainments.

This old custom is concerned with the rights of the villagers to gather wood in Grovely Forest.

## *May 29th*
### Oak-Apple Day

A number of ceremonies commemorate the return of Charles II to this country after his long exile. People everywhere were tired of the joyless rule of the Puritans under the Commonwealth and so the restoration of the monarchy was greeted with jubilation. Many local festivities were moved to this day as a sign of loyalty, particularly those which were associated with greenery. This was because the one thing that caught the popular imagination was the fact that when the Roundheads were searching for Charles II after the battle of Boscobel, he hid in an oak tree.

## *May 29th*
### Founder's Day
### London: Royal Hospital

Charles II founded a 'hostel or guest-house for worthy veterans of the Army' in 1682. There is a statue of him by Grinling Gibbons in the centre of the main court. This is decorated with oak-leaves and the veterans, dressed in their famous scarlet uniforms, parade, are inspected, and then march past to military music. Three cheers are given to 'King Charles, our pious Founder', the parade is dismissed and the pensioners receive a special allowance of beer and plum pudding.

## *May 29th*
### Garland King
### Castleton, Derbyshire

This is a very old custom which has probably been transferred from Old May Day to celebrate the restoration of Charles II.

The Garland King, a man who rides on a horse, wears a large wooden frame covered with greenery and flowers. This almost completely covers the top half of his body, so that his face is unrecognizable. On the very top of the garland is a special nosegay called the Queen. He and his Queen are led through the town accompanied by the town band, Morris dancers and others. The procession perambulates round the town to the market place. At the church the garland is removed, the posy detached, and the garland is then hoisted to the top of the tower while the posy is laid at the foor of the War Memorial.

*May 29th*
**Remembrance Day**
**Northampton, Northamptonshire**
Northampton has a special reason to remember Charles II. In 1675 there was a disastrous fire that destroyed a large part of the town. The king gave 1000 tons of timber to help rebuild it, and he also excused the town from paying the chimney tax for seven years.

You'll see the Mayor and Corporation, all carrying bunches of oak-apples and gilded leaves, leading a procession from the Town Hall to All Saints' Church for a service. The statue of Charles II in the church is decorated with oak sprigs.

*May 29th*
**Lord Leycester Hospital's Celebration**
**Warwick, Warwickshire**
Leycester Hospital is a hospital for army veterans which is actually older than London's Royal Hospital. Here the rooms are decorated with oak-leaves and branches, and there is a special allowance of food and drink for the Brethren. They are also given 15p, and the Master of the Hospital gets 5p. This is because there were once twelve of the Brethren who were sorry for the master because he used to receive nothing at all, so they each contributed one old penny from their small allowance to cheer him up and, as you know, twelve old pennies now total 5p.

*May 29th*
**Worcester Royalist Day**
**Worcester, Hereford and Worcester**
The battle of Worcester which the Royalists lost in 1651 really marked the end of the Civil War. Worcester remem-

bers both this and the Restoration by decorating the Guild Hall gates with branches and greenery and by holding a commemorative service.

*May: moveable*
**Mayoring Day**
**Rye, East Sussex**
This beautiful town used to be an important port, but it is now inland. At one time it had the privilege of minting its own coins, and this occasion is a reminder of those times. At 12 am the Mayor and other officials throw hot pennies from their balcony to a crowd waiting below. As you can imagine, it's the children who manage to pocket most of them.

*May: moveable (sometimes early June)*
**Beating the Retreat**
**London: Horse Guards**
The title of this ceremony, performed by the army or the Royal Marines, makes it seem if the troops are running away. Actually it's a reminder of the days when the armed forces signalled the arrival of dusk and the retreat of daylight, usually about half an hour before sunset.

It is now a splendid occasion, usually performed by the Household Division with a parade, mounted bands, trumpeters and drummers. After the actual parade you'll hear the Last Post sounded, and then the actual beating of the retreat. About a couple of weeks later this ceremony is repeated, but it is performed by a different branch of the services. Every third year the Royal Marines carry out the duties in honour of Prince Philip's birthday since he is their Captain General.

*May: moveable (Spring Bank Holiday Monday)*
**Morris Thanksgiving**
**Charing, Kent**
In the parish church at 11 am a service is held to give thanks for the Morris. The congregation will consist of East Kent Morris Men and probably some visiting Morris dancers, all wearing their traditional clothes. Performances are given afterwards.

*May: moveable (Spring Bank Holiday Monday)*
**Cheese Rolling**
**Birdlip, Gloucestershire**

It doesn't seem very likely, but it seems that by rolling cheeses down Cooper's Hill the local people are maintaining their ancient grazing rights.

Whatever the reason, it's an extraordinary custom. In the late afternoon or early evening people collect on the hill, waiting for the start. The starter rolls the first cheese down on the count of three while everyone waits tensely for the shout of 'Four!' Off they hurtle down the hill trying to catch the cheese. The winner gets a small cash prize as well. This race is followed by others, including one for girls.

*May: moveable (Spring Bank Holiday Monday)*
**Wool Race**
**Tetbury, Gloucestershire**
Tetbury used to be one of the richest wool towns in the Cotswolds. As a reminder of its past teams compete in carrying half-hundredweight sacks of wool up and down Gumstool Hill.

*May: moveable (Spring Bank Holiday Monday)*
**East Land Auction**
**Eastgate, Bourne, Lincolnshire**
In 1770 Richard Clay left a piece of land, the Whitbread Meadows, so that the rent could be used to buy bread for the inhabitants of the village. At 7 pm an auctioneer starts

boys running a fixed distance. As soon as they have started, he asks those present to start bidding. As bids can only be made while the boys are actually running, bidding becomes brisk. As they return, the hammer goes down, and the last person to make a bid wins the right to pay rent on the meadows for the next year.

## Whitsun

*May: moveable*
Whitsun comes seven weeks after Easter. Most parishes used to hold a Church Ale, or feast, to raise money for the church and to provide a social occasion for its parishioners. Money raised by the feast helped not only the church but also the poor. There were games, competitions, singing and dancing, usually presided over by a Lord and Lady of the Ale, but gradually this pleasant custom died out and had vanished by the middle of the 19th century.

Many of the customs that used to take place on Whit Sunday or Whit Monday have now been transferred to Spring Bank Holiday Sunday and Monday, so you must check up if you want to see something in particular. Generally speaking, ceremonies connected with the church or old charities will still take place on the same day, but find out before you make a journey.

*May: moveable (Whit Sunday)*
### Rush-strewing
### Bristol, Avon
At the end of the 13th century the Lord Mayor of Bristol left some property so that money would be provided for three sermons to be preached in St Mary Radcliffe at Pentecost before the Lord Mayor. Some of the money was to be used for rush-strewing and also for the pealing of the bells (*see* p 93).

The church is still strewn with rushes and a bouquet of flowers placed on each seat. Preceded by his Sword Bearer, the Lord Mayor and a procession of other dignitaries enter the church to be greeted by the Bishop of Bristol. There has been one change, though. The three sermons have been cut down to one.

*May: moveable (Whit Sunday)*
### Distribution of Bread and Cheese
### St Briavels, Gloucestershire
A curious custom takes place in this small village in the Forest of Dean. Bread and cheese are scrambled for after the evening service on Whit Sunday. The food is carried in baskets along a lane to a high stone wall where it is tossed to the villagers. It is said that this act maintains their rights of grazing and wood cutting in Hudnall's Wood and that these privileges date back to the 13th century.

*May: moveable (Whit Monday)*
### Morris Dancers
### Bampton, Oxfordshire
Morris dancing goes on from early morning in the streets of Bampton. The dancers carry with them a ritual cake stuck on the point of a decorated sword.

*May: moveable (Whit Monday)*
### Dicing for Bibles
### St Ives, Cambridgeshire
Six Bibles are diced for by twelve children, half of them members of the Church of England and the others of the Nonconformist Church. This bequest came from Dr Robert Wilde who died in 1675 leaving a piece of land still called Bible Orchard to provide the necessary funds.

*May: moveable (Whit Monday or during Whit week)*
### Well-Dressing
### Wirksworth, Derbyshire
It's not the wells that are dressed in Wirksworth, but the places where public taps used to stand when water was first laid on. It is the occasion for the town's festival (*see* p 93).

*May: moveable (Whit Monday)*
### Ram Roasting Fair
### Kingsteignton, Devon
The decorated carcass of a male lamb is carried through the streets. While it is being roasted, and this takes about four hours, everyone takes part in games and dancing, and then those that are lucky enough have a piece of roast lamb.

For centuries the main water supply here was a stream. One day it dried up. According to one story, a priest said that all should pray for the restoration of the water. Everyone did, water reappeared, and the villagers sacrificed a lamb in gratitude. Another story says that because the water dried up a lamb was sacrificied, and miraculously, it flowed again. From that time onwards a live lamb was first paraded through the streets, but towards the end of the 19th century it was decided to butcher the lamb first.

*May: moveable (Whit Monday)*
**Corby Pole Fair**
**Corby, Northamptonshire**
You won't have long to wait to go to Corby Pole Fair. It only takes place every twenty years, but the next one is due in 1982 (*see* p 92).

The people of Corby were given special privileges by Queen Elizabeth in 1585. Apparently, when out riding one day, her horse bolted and she went head over heels into a bog, and she was rescued by Corby men who working in nearby fields.

This isn't the reason why Corby holds this unique fair, but it's an interesting story.

Before the fun begins, all roads leading into the town are closed. Any travellers wanting to pass are asked to pay a toll. If they refuse, they are carried off, the men astride a pole, and the women in chairs. Off they go to the stocks, and there they asked yet again to pay the toll. If they refuse they are locked in the stocks until they pay up.

The old rights and privileges aren't forgotten. At the opening ceremony of the fair the charter is read aloud.

*May: moveable (Whit Monday, or near)*
**Greenhill Bower and Court of Array**
**Lichfield, Staffordshire**
This is a mixture of two old customs. In the Middle Ages the guilds of the city met together, each carrying symbols of their trade and all with garlands of flowers as well as statues of their patron saints. At the Court of Array there was an inspection and a parade of the town's suits of armour. By the 15th century the city was responsible for providing

twelve suits of chain-armour and two of knight's armour as its share of the country's defences. Somehow these two occasions became mixed up. There are processions, flowers, a pleasure fair, the inspection of the remaining suits of armour, and other events. Oddly enough, the procession is always led by a man on a horse smoking a large cigar.

*May: moveable*
**Rogationtide and Ascension Day**

These are Christian festivals and, like so many others, they do not come on a special date.

Ascension Day is the day when Christians celebrate the ascension of Christ. Rogation Sunday is the Sunday before Ascension Day, and Rogationtide includes the Monday, Tuesday and Wednesday. These days were times when God's blessing was asked upon newly sown crops or on fishing waters.

Parish boundaries were also marked at these times, and many places still have processions which go round inspecting or beating them. The reason for this was that when there were hardly any maps the best way of remembering the boundaries was by walking round the area so that everyone knew where they were. Young people had a particularly rough time since they usually had to do the really tough jobs like stumbling through streams or climbing over walls.

*May: moveable (Wednesday before Ascension Eve)*
**Blessing the Sea**
**Hastings, East Sussex**
The ceremony of blessing the sea takes place here. The rectors of All Saints' Church and St Clement's Church conduct a service from the Stade, near the harbour, using a lifeboat as a pulpit.

*May: moveable (Ascension Eve)*
**Planting the Penny Hedge**
**Whitby, North Yorkshire**
This is a penance for a crime committed in 1159. Three men were out hunting one day, and pursued a wild boar into woods belonging to the Abbott of Whitby. The boar,

now wounded and exhausted, took refuge in the cell of a hermit who shut the door in the face of the hunters. Furious at being deprived of their prey, the hunters burst in and wounded the hermit so badly that he was clearly dying. The hermit asked to see his murderers and the Abbot before he died, and he begged that they should be allowed to live and not executed provided they and their descendants performed a penance for ever.

At sunrise they had to go to Stray-head Wood and cut stakes. These were carried to Whitby harbour and planted at the water's edge in a kind of fence which had to be strong enough to withstand three consecutive tides. While this was all going on the Abbot's bailiff had to sound his horn and shout 'Out upon you'. If you go to watch, don't imagine that those planting the hedge are descendants of the murderers. The ceremony is performed by the tenant of the land.

*May: moveable (Ascension Day, every two years)*
**Beating the Bounds**
**London: Queen's Chapel of the Savoy**
Beating the bounds of the Liberty of the Savoy takes some time since it wanders round a number of streets. Watch the procession and see the fun as two choirboys are bumped — one close to Cleopatra's Needle and the other in Temple Gardens. *See* Beating the Bounds p 90.


# June

*June: moveable (Ascension Day every third year)*
**Beating the Bounds**
**London: Tower of London**
Beating the Bounds takes some time here, since there are thirty-one boundaries to be marked. There is a big procession led by the Resident Governor in full dress, Yeoman Warders dressed in their best, other officials, the clergy and the choristers. At each of the marks the Chaplain shouts, 'Cursed is he who removeth his neighbour's land mark!'

The Chief Warder responds with 'Whack it, boys, whack it!' and the choirboys hit the mark energetically with willow wands. *See* Beating the Bounds p 90.

*June: moveable (Ascension Day)*
**Beating the Bounds**
**Lichfield, Staffordshire**
Here the clergy and choir from the Cathedral carry elm boughs. They stop at eight fixed points on their journey and read the Bible and sing a psalm. On their return to the Cathedral they leave the elm boughs by the font (*see* p 90).

*June: moveable (Ascension Day)*
**Well-Dressing**
**Tissington, Derbyshire**
There are five wells in Tissington. Some people believe that the custom of dressing them was the result of the fact that during the 17th century when there was a very severe drought, Tissington's wells continued to supply water so that people came from miles around to collect it. Others think that the custom started after the Black Death of 1348-1349. People all over the country suffered, and there were many deaths. About half of Derbyshire died, but not one in Tissington, due to the purity of the water it was believed. Whatever the reason, it is well worth making a journey to admire the wells. There is first a service of thanksgiving in the church, and then a procession goes to each well in turn where it is blessed.

*June: moveable*
**Isra'Wal Mi'raj**
Muslims remember in their prayers the night journey of the prophet Muhammad from Mecca to Jerusalem, and his ascent to heaven.

*June: moveable*
**Feast of Weeks**
This Jewish festival comes seven weeks after Passover. It celebrates the time when the Jews received the Ten Commandments on Mount Sinai. If you go into a synagogue on this day you will find it decorated with flowers and plants

since it is also the feast of the harvest and the day of the first fruit offering.

## June: moveable
### Ratha Yatra
This is a Hindu festival in honour of Jagannath, the Lord of the Universe. In Puri in India, where there is a superb temple built for him, gigantic, decorated cars are dragged through the streets by thousands of pilgrims.

## June: usually first Sunday
### Mourne Wall Walk
### Mourne, Co Down
Do you fancy yourself as a walker? Yes? Well, get in touch with the Youth Hostels Association in Dublin. This walking event over a 35 kilometre (22 mile) course following the line of a boundary wall over the highest peaks of Mourne Mountains attracts about two thousand people. It's non-competitive, but you do receive a certificate if you manage it — and you will have earned it!

## June: first Tuesday
### Bubble Sermon
### London: St Martin-within-Ludgate Church
If you go to Stationers' Hall you will see members of the Stationers' Company as they make their way to the church to listen to the Bubble Sermon. One of their members, Richard Johnson, who died in the 18th century, left money for the poor of the Company on condition that a sermon should be preached annually on this day. However, he stipulated that the sermon always had to have the same theme — life is just a bubble.

## June: first week
### Clock Race
### Bideford, Devon
This is a race which has been going on for well over fifty years. The parish clock takes very nearly twenty-two seconds to strike eight, and so, just before the hour, runners line up at one end of the twenty-four arched bridge over the River Torridge. At the first stroke, off they go, each

person trying to get to the other side before the clock has finished striking.

*June: Thursday, Friday, Saturday in first full week*
**Common Riding**
**Selkirk, Borders**
The Scots were beaten at the battle of Flodden in 1513. Tradition says that only one man who left Selkirk to fight the English returned. He carried a captured English banner, and this he cast silently in the street. Common Riding commemorates this event.

On the Thursday evening there is the Crying of the Burley by the Burgh officer who is dressed in knee breeches and wears a high hat. Then there is the bussing of the flags when girls kiss the standards which are to be carried by horsemen on the following day.

Flutes and drums wake the citizens at 4 o'clock the next morning. People rush onto the streets and within a short time they are all singing and dancing. At about 6.30 the Provost's lady busses the Burgh Flag and hands it to the Standard Bearer. Off goes a large company of horsemen, all carrying pennants. Led by the Standard Bearer, they ride the bounds and then, on their return, they Cast the Colours. The Standard Bearer climbs onto a scarlet dais and as the Burgh band plays 'Up wi' the Souters o' Selkirk', he raises the silken flag and casts it to and fro and round and round keeping perfect time. Then four more Standard Bearers appear, each in turn casting his flag. There is silence for a minute or so while people remember the dead, and then the band plays 'The Liltin'.

Selkirk has more to offer — horse races, the Common Riding Ball and, on the Saturday, a gymkhana, Highland dancing, sports and a fair (*see* p 90).

*June: Thursday, Friday in first full week*
**Common Riding**
**Hawick, Borders**
Just one year after the battle of Flodden the men of Hawick scored a victory over the English when they surprised a number of solidiers at Hornshole, a pool outside the town. There was a fight, the English were routed, and

the men of Hawick brought home the gold and blue English banner in triumph.

Now, on the Thursday evening the flag is bussed by the Cornet's Lass who ties blue and gold ribbons to it. The standard is handed over to the Cornet who is ordered to return it 'unsullied and unstained'. At this everyone bursts into 'Terribus' a local song with a rousing chorus. Then the Cornet parades through the town displaying the flag to the crowds.

On the following morning at 6 o'clock the drum and fife band, accompanied by officers, sets out to wake up the town. Then there is the curious ceremony of taking snuff. At about 8.45 the Cornet and well over a hundred other riders, all wearing oak leaves, sets off for St Leonard's. On the way they all stop for the chase, a re-enactment of the original capture of the flag. Then comes the riding of the marches when the racecourse is visited and racing takes place. The afternoon is spent in sports and games, and at the end of the day are held the Cornet's Dinner and Common Riding Ball.

There are more ceremonies the next day when wreaths are laid at the War Memorial and the flag is returned to the Provost. Everyone enjoys more sports and, in the evening, all the fun of the fair (see p 90).

*June: second Friday*
**Whipman's Festival**
**West Linton, Borders**
The whipmen were carters and ploughmen who used to have an annual sports day. This simple occasion has turned into an important event.

On this day the retiring Whipman formally hands his Whipman's Flag to the President, the proclamation is read, and the new Whipman is invested with his sash and handed the Flag. All join in the singing of the Installation Song. A procession including the band, the Whipman and his supporters, all on horseback, and accompanied by decorated vehicles and people in fancy-dress makes its way to the Lower Green where the Whipman's Reel is danced.

The following day brings a great burst of activity — sports, dancing, games and a concert.

*June: second Saturday*
**Trooping of the Colour**
**London: Horse Guards**
This really impressive military parade is performed in honour of the Queen's official birthday. The Queen rides at the head of a procession from Buckingham Palace to the Horse Guards where she inspects the Guards. Then comes the trooping ceremony with its precision marching to military bands and with the Queen taking the salute. At the end of this parade which really lasts quite a long time, the Queen leads the way back to Buckingham Palace at the head of the Guards.

This custom goes back to the time when the British army, like all armies at the time, had a lot of mercenaries in it — that is, people from different countries who fought only for money. Many of these knew very little English. This was a problem, particularly in the heat of battle when they might not understand the orders being given. So, the regimental flag was paraded in front of them so that it became familiar, and it then acted as a rallying point in battle.

It's difficult to get a ticket for this occasion, but you can get a marvellous view of the procession from the Mall, and it is possible to obtain tickets for the two rehearsals — the first is free, the second is not. Write to the Brigade Major, Household Division, Whitehall, London SW1 if you want to go.

*June 17th (or near)*
**Rushbearing**
**Haworth, West Yorkshire**
A small procession of the choir and church members leave the rectory for the church. Some of the young children carry rushes which have been collected from the moors and these are scattered in the aisles of the church (*see* p 93).

*June: second Saturday*
**Abinger Common Medieval Fair**
**Abinger, Surrey**
This is a really good fair with many people dressed up in medieval clothes. There's a procession led by riders on

horseback, the crowning of the Queen, a maypole and Morris dancing — in fact, there's all the fun of the fair.

This fair recalls the time when pilgrims went on foot to visit the tomb of St Thomas à Becket at Canterbury. Abinger was one of the places where these pilgrims stopped overnight.

*June 20th (or near)*
**Mayor of Ock Street**
**Abingdon, Oxfordshire**
On St Edmund's Day an ox used to be roasted and the meat given to the poor. Round about 1700 there was a sudden brawl about who should have the horns of the beast, and the men from up-town fought it out with the men of down-town. At the end of it a Morris dancer called Hemmings was in possession of the horns and was proudly proclaimed the Mayor of Ock Street.

Today a Mayor is still elected by the people of Ock Street. At 4 pm the votes are counted. The new Mayor has a drink from his mace — actually a wooden bowl with a silver rim — and he is carried through the streets by the Abingdon Morris Dancers, led by the hornbearer who carries a pole with the horns of an ox on top. Throughout the evening the Morris Dancers, all wearing top hats, white shirts and black breeches with bells and ribbons, dance outside the pubs and in the market place. Both the Mayor and the mace go with them. The mace is refilled and emptied quite frequently — after all, dancing is thirsty work.

*June 23rd*
**Peace and Good Neighbourhood Dinner**
**Kidderminster, Hereford and Worcester**
About five hundred years ago a woman left some money to be spent on the inhabitants of Church Street. It provided a loaf for each child who was born in or who was living in the street on Midsummer Eve. Everyone looked forward to Farthing Loaf Day. Later this sum of money was increased so that each child and each spinster could have plum cake as well. The men received tobacco and ale.

As a result of these bequests, there is now an annual dinner at which the Chairman tries to get neighbours who might have quarrelled to make it up by giving a toast of 'Peace and Good Neighbourhood'.

*June 23rd*
**Midsummer Eve Bonfires**
**Cornwall**

Before Christian times, people used to light fires on midsummer eve because the following day the sun would be at its highest in the sky. In doing this they hoped to encourage the sun not to go away but to stay longer and warm the earth. There was another purpose. These fires would also drive away evil.

In Cornwall material for the bonfires was collected from May onwards. On Midsummer Eve flags were raised over mines, and the miners climbed rocky outcrops to sound the midsummer holes. These were holes drilled in the rocks, packed with gunpowder, and fired.

Nowadays in Cornwall a chain of bonfires blazes across the county. Each fire is blessed in Cornish, the Lady of the Flowers tosses wild flowers and herbs onto it, and sometimes young couples jump hand in hand across the flames to bring good luck in the coming year.

*June 23rd*
**The Witch's Bonfire**
**St Cleer, Cornwall**
This particular Midsummer Eve bonfire has a special purpose. It is carefully built and then a witch's hat and broomstick are put on top. The fire is lit, herbs and flowers are

tossed in, and a new sickle is thrown on to the flames. After all this it would be a very foolhardy witch who approached St Cleer.

## *June 24th*
## Election of Sheriffs
## London: Guildhall

The Liverymen of the City of London Guilds meet at Common Hall to elect two sheriffs and other officers for the coming year. The Lord Mayor and his officers arrive and sit on a dais strewn with herbs, with the mace and sword placed in front of them. The Lord Mayor, the City Marshall, the Sword-Bearer, the Recorder, the Town Clerk, and any Alderman who has already been a Sheriff leave the room. The mace is left behind as a symbol of the authority of the Lord Mayor. Those left behind elect the new Sheriffs. The choice is important for only Sheriffs are eligible to be Lord Mayor of London some time in the future.

## *June 24th (Thursday nearest)*
## Well Dressing
## Buxton, Derbyshire

The water in St Anne's Well in Buxton was thought to have healing powers in medieval times. A statue was found in the well and the people believed it was one of St Anne, so they built a little chapel for it close to the well. During the Reformation this chapel was destroyed. However, St Anne is still remembered when her well is dressed by the people of Buxton (*see* p 93).

## *June 24th or near*
## Presentation of the Knollys Rose
## London: Mansion House

About six hundred years ago Lady Constance Knollys must have been feeling rather bored. After all, her husband had been away fighting the French for some time. Then something captured her interest. She lived in Seething Lane and a piece of land just across the road suddenly came up for sale. She promptly bought it and turned it into a rose garden. But then a problem arose. Seething Lane, like every other street in London, was muddy and often smelly. Lady

Constance didn't fancy getting her feet dirty every time she wanted to go into her rose garden, so she simply built herself a bridge from the house to the garden.

However, when her husband came home from the war, he was horrified to discovered that she hadn't bothered to get planning permission. He was charged with the offence and found guilty, but in view of his distinguished service in the field the Lord Mayor decided to be lenient. He fined him, but the fine was a single red rose to be presented annually to the Lord Mayor. And so it still is. The rose is presented on a blue altar cushion to the Lord Mayor by the churchwardens of All Hallows Barking by the Tower — and a member of the Knollys family still attends the ceremony.

*June 29th (Sunday following)*
**Rushbearing**
**Wingrave, Buckinghamshire**
Many years ago an old lady lost her way one night. Stumbling around in the dark, and uncertain which way to go, she suddenly heard the sound of the bells of St Peter and St Paul's Church in Wingrave. In gratitude she left a field to the parish. Fresh hay from this field is still strewn in the church and the income from the rent of this field is used to renew the church hassocks. *See* Rushbearing p 93.

*June 29th*
**Rushbearing**
**Warcop, Cumbria**
A procession makes its way to the church, the boys carrying small crosses made of rushes, and the girls wearing floral crowns on their heads. These are placed around the altar during the service and afterwards they are hung over the main door of the church until St Peter's day comes round the following year (*see* p 93).

*June: usually last Friday (sometimes first Friday in July)*
**Braw Lads Gathering**
**Galashiels, Borders**
This commemorates a number of events — the defeat of an English raiding party, the first ceremony on Scottish soil enacted in front of Margaret Tudor who married King

James IV of Scotland, and the foundation of the Burgh of Galashiels in 1599. It is also a reminder of the Galashiels Fair which was held to form a kind of rallying point for the residents of the district — and if that wasn't enough, it is also the Common Riding (see p 90).

Preparations for this festival start early. Each of the five wards elects a Braw Lad and Braw Lassie, and from these a Chief Braw Lad and Lassie are chosen. Events include the presentation of earth and stone to them, the handing over of the Burgh flag by the Provost, and the Riding. There is also dancing, racing, both on horseback and on foot, and other entertainments.

*June: last Saturday and first week in July*
**Wakes and Well Dressing**
**Hope, Derbyshire**
Each year the Wakes and Well Dressing starts on the last Saturday in June with the crowning of the Wakes Queen, fancy-dress parades, floats in the street, and so on. To commemorate St Peter's day, there is a flower festival and a display of church treasures in the parish church (*see* p 93).

*June: third week*
**Beltane Festival**
**Peebles, Borders**
Beltane was the ancient Celtic May Day. At Peebles this festival goes back hundreds of years to a fair established during the reign of Robert the Bruce. It starts on the Sunday with a service, and on the Wednesday you can see the Cornet's Canter to Neidpath Castle and the riding of the marches (*see* p 90). Then comes the dancing of the Cornet's Reel in Tontine Square and later on the Cornet's Canter Dance which spills into the streets.

On the following day there is the Cornet's Walk and the Beltane Concert, and there are more festivities on the Friday.

Saturday is the actual Beltane Festival and it is a great day for the children. The fair is proclaimed at the Mercat Cross, the Beltane Queen's Standard Bearer leads up to four hundred children, all in fancy dress to the cross, and then, amid great ceremony, the Queen is crowned. A huge procession forms and riders, bands, all the children and hundreds of people march to the War Memorial where wreaths are laid and the pipes play 'Flowers of the Forest'. Then there are sports and the whole festival is brought to an end with the Beating of the Retreat.

# July

*July: first week*
**Reiver's Week**
**Duns, Borders**
The Sunday before the beginning of Reiver's Week is actually the start of the festivities, for this is when the Reiver and his Lass, the Wynsome Mayde o' Duns, the Provost and other officials attend a service in the old parish church. On the following evening the Reiver and his Lass are installed. The Provost hands the Reiver the Burgh Standard, and he leads a horse-back procession.

Throughout the week there are plenty of things to see and do. There's the crowning of the Wynsome Mayde, the riding of the bounds (*see* p 90), Maypole dancing, pageants, a torchlight procession with thousands carrying flickering torches, and a wild game of handball played between the married and the single men. What with all of this, and concerts, races, exhibitions, and horse-jumping, you'll go home exhausted but happy.

*July 4th*
**Midsummer Eve Bonfire**
**Whalton, Northumberland**
It seems that the people of Whalton decided to have nothing to do with the new calendar when it was introduced, for they have their Midsummer bonfire on old Midsummer Eve. There's a splendid blaze, children dance round the flames, and later on they scramble for sweets. *See* The Old Calendar, p 93.

## July 5th
### Tynwald Ceremony
### St John's, Isle of Man

The Isle of Man is an ancient kingdom with its own government which makes its own laws, levies its own taxes, and decides upon its own expenditure. The Tynwald is the Manx Parliament, traditionally founded by King Orry. It is certainly one of the world's oldest legislative assemblies.

On old Midsummer Day there is a short service and a procession to Tynwald Hill, a step-mound built from earth collected in each of the seventeen parishes. People sit or stand at various levels on the hill, a summary of the laws passed is read in both Manx and English, everyone gives three cheers, and the procession returns to St John's.

## July: Wednesday in second week
### Pretty Maid Ceremony
### Holsworthy, Devon

The second week in July is St Peter's Fair week. On the Wednesday there is a very pleasant little ceremony when a single maid, noted for her looks, gentleness, and quietness, is chosen to receive a small sum of money. The announcement is made from the west door of the church.

## July 8th and 9th
### Burry Man and Ferry Fair
### South Queensferry, Lothian

The Ferry Fair is held on July 9th but the mysterious Burry Man appears on the previous day. He wears close-fitting clothes which are completely covered with the burrs of thistles and his head is covered with a head-dress decorated with flowers and more burrs. He is completely unrecognizable. He holds a decorated staff in each of his hands and, accompanied by two attendants, he moves slowly through the town, stopping silently at house after house. Wherever he goes he is greeted with respect and money is given to his attendants. He brings luck, but nothing is known of his origin.

## July: moveable
### Lailatul Bara'ah
Muslims remember the Ascension of the Prophet Muhammad.

*July 12th*
**Battle of the Boyne Celebrations**
**Northern Ireland**
In 1688 James II fled from England after William of Orange, who had been invited to take the throne by Whig and Tory leaders, landed. James II headed a rising in Ireland, but in 1690 he was defeated by William of Orange, now William III, at the Battle of the Boyne. Celebrations are held in many parts of Northern Ireland with bands, banners, marches, and services of the Orange Order.

*July 13th*
**Sham Fight**
**Scarva, Co Down**
Scarva was the site of William III's camp before the Battle of the Boyne. A huge crowd gathers here to watch a colourful display with bands, and then they watch local people, all dressed in costume, re-enact the battle. There are accounts of the sham fight going back to 1835 but it probably dates from the late 18th century. Note that if July 13th falls on a Sunday the ceremony takes place on the following day.

*July 19th*
**Little Edith's Treat**
**Piddinghoe, East Sussex**
A bequest was made so that there could be a church service, races and tea, all in memory of little Edith Croft who died in 1869 aged three months.

*July 19th: (Tuesday and Wednesday following)*
**Honiton Fair**
**Honiton, Devon**
This fair began in 1257 and was originally held at Whitsuntide. It is opened by the Town Crier who holds a staff with a gilt glove fixed to the top of it. He shouts 'Oyez! Oyez! Oyez! The glove is up and the fair has begun! No man shall be arrested until the glove is taken down! God save the Queen!' The glove is then taken to the King's Arms and the pole put on the balcony while down below children, often with rags wrapped round their hands, wait eagerly for a shower of hot pennies to be thrown to them.

*July: third week, Thursday, Friday, Saturday*
## Cleiking the Devil
### Innerleithen, Borders

St Ronan, a 7th century monk, got the better of the Devil when they were having a tussle. It might have been a bit unsporting, but he hooked or 'cleiked' the Devil's hind leg with his shepherd's crook, and so forced him to howl for mercy.

The celebrations begin on the Thursday evening with the installation of the Standard Bearer and his Lass. Then there is a procession to St Ronan's Well and later a service at the War Memorial.

The next evening there is a procession of white-robed monks, St Ronan and the Lantern-Bearer in the Memorial Hall where the new St Ronan is given the Cleikum Crozier and a gold medal, a concert, an address and the showing of the standard, and a tableau. Then there is a torchlight procession to the Runic Cross at Innerleithen church. Here an account of the legend is given and St Ronan drinks water from St Ronan's Well. The procession reforms and, followed by singing, dancing and cheering crowds, returns.

At 11 am the next day there is a flower parade with hundreds of children, St Ronan, his monks, the Standard Bearer, the Lantern Bearer and other officials taking part. Most important of all, an effigy of the Devil goes with them. During the day there are the St Ronan's Border Games and then, as evening draws on, St Ronan and his followers, led by pipers, mount Caerlee. There's a display of fireworks, St Ronan lights the bonfire, and then he lifts the Devil high in the air and flings him into the flames — the Devil has been successfully cleiked once again.

*July 25th*
## The Knill Games
### St Ives, Cornwall

Go to St Ives in 1981 to see the most amazing sight. You'll find a curious group of people gathered together at Knill's Steeple, on the top of Worvas Hill. You'll see ten small girls each under the age of ten, dressed in white and wearing white cockades, a fiddler, two widows over the age of 64, the best knitter of fishing nets, the best curer and the best packer of pilchards, and various others. They are part of a large procession, led by the Mayor, which has climbed the hill from St Ives.

John Knill, the Collector of Customs from 1762-82, wanted to make sure that he was remembered after his death, so he left a number of curious bequests. These are distributed after the ten little girls have danced round the monument for not less than fifteen minutes and have sung the hymn known as 'the Old Hundredth' to the tune used in the parish church in John Knill's time.

What is even odder, is the fact that although he built the Steeple to be his own mausoleum, John Knill isn't actually buried there.

This custom takes place every five years, so if you miss it, you'll have to wait until 1986 to see it.

*July 25th*
**Horn Fair**
**Ebernoe, Sussex**
This is an extraordinary custom which combines the annual roasting of a horned sheep with cricket. Each year the Ebernoe team challenges another team to a cricket match. While this is being played, a horned sheep is roasted whole in a pit of embers with the horns sticking out over the end of the pit so that they won't be burned. At the end of the game the head and horns are presented to the winners of the match.

*July: third week*
**Tweedmouth Feast Week**
**Berwick upon Tweed, Northumberland**
This was a charter fair in medieval times (*see* p 90). Now there is a week-long festival with music, dancing, exhibitions, sports and social activities. If you arrive on the Thursday preceding this week of entertainment you will see the crowning of the Salmon Queen.

*July 26th (or nearest Saturday)*
**Rushbearing**
**Ambleside, Cumbria**
Here you will see a large procession consisting mainly of

children wending its way through the town to the church.
They carry garlands of flowers or rushes and flowers woven
into intricate symbols such as harps and crosses. There are
two huge rush pillars, too, each of them up to 3 metres
(10 feet) high. These are taken into the church. There is a
service and afterwards the children enjoy sticky gingerbread.
*See* p 93.

*July: moveable*
### Ramadan
During the month of Ramadan Muslims fast and read a part
of the Koran, their holy book, each day. Muslims don't
actually have nothing to eat for the whole 28 days — that
would make them ill — but they do fast perhaps one day in
three, or on alternate days. At the end of the month there is a
three-day festival, known as 'The feast of the breaking of
the fast'. Ramadan was chosen as the month for fasting
because it includes the 'Night of Power' — the night during
which the Prophet Muhammad first received the message
from God via the Angel Gabriel.

*July: last week (and first week of August)*
### St Wilfred's Fair
**Ripon, North Yorkshire**
A great deal goes on during this festival fortnight — games,
horse racing, shooting, swimming and various tournaments —
but the most important day is the Saturday before the first
Monday in August. This is the St Wilfred Procession which
celebrates the return of St Wilfred from exile in AD 686.
At one time his statue was taken out of the city on one
day and paraded triumphantly through the city on the next,
but nowadays a local man dressed as St Wilfred and riding
a horse heads a procession of bands, carnival floats, and so
on.

*July: towards the end of the month*
### Swan Upping
**London: River Thames up to Henley**
This is the time when all the new cygnets on the River
Thames between London Bridge and Henley are rounded up
and marked to show who they belong to. Parent birds with

a nick on both sides of the beak belong to the Vintners' Company, those with one nick only are owned by the Dyers' Company, and those with unmarked beaks are the Queen's. If the baby swans are of mixed parentage, half receive the mother's mark, and the others the father's. Any odd cygnets are marked like their fathers.

Quite a procession forms up for swan-upping. The Queen's Swan Keeper and the Swan Masters of the Companies all wear distinctive uniforms, and the oarsmen wear red, white and blue sweaters. Look at the coats of arms on the skiffs. Those belonging to the Queen fly two flags each, one with her initials and a crown, the other with a swan on it. The boats belonging to the Vintners' and the Dyers' Companies carry flags displaying their arms.

*July: moveable*
**Admiralty Court**
**Rochester, Kent**
The Admiralty Court takes place on a lighter moored to Rochester Pier and is presided over by the Mayor who is also the Admiral. There is first a procession of the Mayor, Alderman and other officials, accompanied by the Water Bailiff who carries a large silver oar as a symbol of his authority. Twelve jurymen are sworn to regulate the oyster and floating fishery for the coming year, and so continue a custom which dates back at least 250 years.

# August

*July or August: moveable*
**Rakshabandhan**
This Hindu festival is a family celebration for brothers and sisters which falls on the day of the full moon in the month of Shravana. Rakshabandhan, or Rakhi, actually means a tie — not the kind for your neck, but for security. Sisters tie coloured cotton or silk wristbands to their brothers' wrists and mark their foreheads in vermilion powder. This is a symbol of success and victory. In return the brothers look after their sisters — lucky girls, they get a present too.

*August 5th*
**Horse Fair**
**Brigg, Humberside**
If you happen to be near Brigg just before this date you'll see gipsies making their way to the town to take part in this annual fair which has been going on for about 700 years. The horses are trotted up and down the streets and you'll know when a deal has been done because you'll see it clinched with a traditional handslap.

*August 5th*
**Rushbearing**
**Grasmere, Cumbria**
Rushes are carried in procession to the church as people sing St Oswald's Hymn and the Rushbearing March (*see* p 93). The rushes are woven into traditional shapes like harps and crosses, St Oswald's crown and his miracle-working hand. Six young girls carry a linen sheet with loose rushes in it. There is a service in the church and gingerbread is handed around afterwards. The rushes are left in the church until the following Monday when the owners collect them and go off for a celebratory tea.

*August: first week*
**Royal National Eisteddfod of Wales**

This competitive festival for musicians and poets takes place alternately on sites in north and south Wales. The aim is to foster the Welsh language and its great cultural tradition. The most important event is the Crowning of the Bard, the highest honour a Welsh poet can attain.

Each festival really starts during the previous one when it is proclaimed by the Arch Druid from a stone circle. The sword of peace is laid before him. He lifts it high for everyone to see and half draws it from its scabbard as he asks in Welsh three times, 'A oes heddwch?' ('Is it peace?'), and the crowd shouts back 'Heddwch!' ('Peace!').

*August: 2nd Monday*
**Deer Roasting**
**Cranham, Gloucestershire**
Cranham must be the only place in the country to have a deer roasting. Local people and invited guests enjoy the feast, the annual tug-of-war between men of the village and those of Upton St Leonards, sports and an annual fair, so there's plenty to see and do.

*August 10th (Wednesday following)*
**Well Dressing**
**Barlow, Derbyshire**
In Barlow it is a pump rather than a well that is dressed. The decorations are in the form of three panels, like a triptych. This village has kept up its well-dressing tradition for well over 140 years without a break (*see* p 93).

*August 12th*
**Relief of 'Derry Celebrations**
**Londonderry, Co Antrim**
This commemorates the relief of 'Derry in 1689. The Jacobite army under Lord Antrim marched on the city but they were thwarted by the apprentice boys who shut the city gates and held it for 105 days. By the time that the siege was lifted over 9000 citizens had died. Celebrations include a procession, a wreath-laying ceremony and a thanksgiving service in St Columb's Cathedral. Note that if the date falls on a Friday, Sunday or a Monday, it is held on the nearest Saturday instead, so make sure of the date before you make a journey.

*August: Monday following Sunday after the 12th*
**Marhamchurch Revels**
**Marhamchurch, Cornwall**
St Marwenne brought Christianity to this Cornish village in the 16th century. She lived in a cell outside the church, and it is on that very spot that Father Time crowns the Queen of the Revels. Once crowned she rides on a white horse to the Revel ground accompanied by attendants and the brass band, and then there's fun for all — Cornish wrestling, dancing, competition, sideshows, and so on.

*August 13th-15th*
**Mitcham Fair**
**Mitcham, Surrey**
At one time Mitcham was famous because of the dealing in cattle and horses that took place there. Now it is just a large pleasure fair which is held on Three Kings Common. It is officially open after a huge golden key has been displayed (*see* p 90).

*August 19th (week including)*
**Coracle Racing**
**Cilgerran, Dyfed**
The coracle was one of the earliest forms of water transport. Anyone taking part in these races must have a coracle made in the traditional manner — a hazel wood frame covered with canvas and pitch. These races which take place on the Saturday end a festive week which includes music, sports, a horticultural show and other activities.

*August 24th*
**Bartlemas Day**
**Sandwich, Kent**
This service marks the anniversary of the massacre of the Huguenots in 1572 and it is also the day when the new master of St Bart's Hospital is appointed. The name of the new master is picked out with a bodkin from a list of almsmen. After the service, which takes place at 11.30, the Mayor and the Trustees watch children race around the chapel. The winner gets a Bart's biscuit. The rest get sticky buns.

*August 24th (Saturday nearest)*
**Bartle's Burning**
**West Wilton, North Yorkshire**
It's not really certain just who Bartle was, but most people think that he was an outlaw who lived in a forest near the village and that he was caught and killed in Grassgill Lane when he was raiding the village. Now his effigy is paraded round the streets and is burned in the evening.

There are lots of other things to do here including a fancy-dress parade, sports and a cottage show.

*August: last consecutive Monday and Tuesday*
**Lammas Fair**
**Ballycastle, Co Antrim**
Although Sir Randal Macdonnell obtained a charter for this fair in 1606, it was probably in existence long before that. It is a tremendous occasion with dealers and farmers buying and selling all sorts of livestock, while people buy fruit and vegetables as well as two specialities — dulse, an edible seaweed, and yellow-man, a peculiar sort of toffee. There's the traditional fun of the fair — strong men, fortune-tellers, conjurors, swings, roundabouts and other amusements. In the evening you'll hear lots of music and be able to watch Irish dancing (*see* p 90).

*August: Late Summer Bank Holiday*
**Portobello West Indian Carnival**
**London: Notting Hill**

For three days over the Bank Holiday the streets around the Portobello Road in Notting Hill resound with the rhythmic beat of West Indian music. Spectators join in the spontaneous dancing and enjoy the non-stop activity of this colourful and lively carnival.

*August: first Saturday after third Monday*
**Marymass Fair**
**Irvine, Strathclyde**
This is a really good fair which includes the crowning of the Marymass Queen at the Mercat Cross, the Marymass races, and the Captain's procession (*see* p 90).

*August: last Sunday*
**Plague Sunday**
**Eyam, Derbyshire**
This commemorates the remarkable heroism of the people of this village in 1665-66. When the plague was at its height in London and thousands were dying, a box of infected clothing reached Eyam from London. Within a short time the plague was rampant in the village. The Rector realized that if the people left the village many of them would take the plague with them and so it would spread through the countryside. He explained this to the villagers, and so they agreed to isolate themselves. The Earl of Devonshire helped by arranging for food and medicine to be taken to Mompesson's Well and left there while the villagers collected it and left money in payment in jars of vinegar. Church services were held in the open air in the dell because it was thought that this might prevent those who were uninfected from coming into close contact with those who might already have the plague. Eventually the plague disappeared, but only forty-one of the villagers were left alive.

Now, on this day, a procession of local people with both Anglican and Nonconformist clergy, led by a band, makes its way to Cucklet Dell where a service is held.

*August: moveable*
**All Souls' Day**
This, like the Christian festival celebrated on November 2nd, is the time when Chinese Buddhists think about the dead.

In particular the Chinese remember those spirits who are homeless or have no descendants to mourn them.

*August: moveable*
**Janam Ashtami**
The Lord Krishna was born at midnight, so Hindus go to temples where they not only pray but they watch people enacting scenes showing moments in his early life.

# September

*September 1st*
**Opening of the Oyster Season**
**Colchester, Essex**
Colchester obtained the oyster fisheries in the River Colne in 1186 from Richard I.

On this day the Mayor, members of the Town Council and of the Fisheries Board go in a fishing smack from Brightlingsea to Pyfleet Creek. The Town Clerk reads a proclamation of 1256 which states Colchester's right to the fisheries and then the Mayor officially opens the season by lowering a trawl and bringing up the first oysters. The Queen's health is drunk and everyone munches his way through a piece of gingerbread.

*September: moveable*
**Idil Fitri**
On the evening of the last day of Ramadam a Muslim priest watches for the rising of the moon. As soon as it appears he announces it and the celebrations begin. The next day Muslims hold open house for all. There is as much food as anyone can eat and gifts of money for visiting children. As many things as possible are bought new for this special occasion.

*September: Monday following the first Sunday after 4th*
**Horn Dance**
**Abbots Bromley, Staffordshire**
Hundreds of people turn up to watch this ancient dance.

Everything about it is mysterious. No one knows what its origins are or where the reindeer horns came from, although carbon testing dates them at 1065. There are six pairs of antlers, three painted blue and the others white, and they weigh from over 7 kilograms (16 pounds) to 11 kilograms (25 pounds) so this is no dance for weaklings.

The dancers, wearing knee breeches, jerkins, stockings and with flat caps on their heads fetch the antlers from the church at about 8.30 am. They are accompanied by a man dressed as Maid Marion, a Fool with a pig's bladder balloon, a Hobby-Horse, a Bowman, a musician who plays an accordion, and a boy with a triangle. They set off on a long and tiring journey round the parish, taking in some outlying farmhouses, visiting as many as possible, for they are luck-bringers. The actual dance takes the form of moving first in a straight line, then a circle and then dividing into three pairs. The two lines move forward looking as if they are going to fight but instead of locking antlers they retreat again, advance and retreat. Occasionally all the groups takes part in the dance, but usually Maid Marion and the Fool collect money. At the end of the day the dancers are back in the main street of the village, tired and thirsty men.

*September 8th (Saturday nearest)*
**Sheriff's Ride**
**Lichfield, Staffordshire**
Under Lichfield's charter of 1553 the Bailiff and Brethren of Lichfield have to elect a Sheriff on July 25th. One of his duties is to go round the city boundaries. So, this is the day when you'll find him on horseback with other riders, ready to trot off on the 38 kilometre (24 mile) journey. They leave the Guildhall at about 11 am, stopping here and there. The city Sword Bearer and the Mace Bearer wait for his return as it's their job to conduct him safely back to the Guildhall. *See* Beating the Bounds, p 90.

*September: second Tuesday*
**Widecombe Fair**
**Widecombe, Devon**
Although according to the song this is the fair that Uncle Tom Cobley was going to, it's a bit of a surprise to find

that the first time this fair was held was in 1850, about fifty years after his death. It's a good, crowded and noisy fair where you can see some Dartmoor sheep and ponies being sold.

*September: second Saturday*
**Great Fair**
**Findon, Sussex**
This is an enormous sheep fair where well over 10,000 sheep might be sold.

*September 12th*
**Stratford Mop Fair**
**Stratford-upon-Avon, Warwickshire**
You're not very likely to find anyone hanging around here with a crook or a milking-pail, but you will see the official opening of the fair by the Mayor, be able to smell and watch the ox being roasted and see the country dancing. Stratford has a Runaway Mop Fair later in the month. *See* p 91.

*September 12th or near*
**Warwick Mop Fair**
**Warwick, Warwickshire**
Like the fair at Stratford-upon-Avon, this is opened by the Mayor. There is an ox-roast, and a great deal of other entertainment goes on. This fair is followed by a Runaway Mop Fair later in the month. *See* p 91.

*September 18th (Saturday nearest)*
**Crab Fair**
**Egremont, Cumbria**
These crabs aren't found in the sea. They are crab apples which are thrown to the crowd and symbolise the largesse distributed by the Lord of the Manor in earlier days. Later on there is the fun of the gurning competition. Competitors put their heads through a horse collar and the person who pulls the most hideous face is the winner.

*September 19th (Sunday nearest)*
**Clipping the Church**
**Painswick, Gloucestershire**
This is a kind of dance round the church and by joining hands the parishioners embrace or clip the church as they move round in a circle. At Painswick there is a procession of children through the town. On reaching the church they form a circle and dance round it three times, advancing and retreating as they go while the Clipping Hymn is sung. Painswick churchyard is famous for its yew trees.

*September 19th (as near as possible)*
**First Fruit Ceremony**
**Richmond, Yorkshire**
The Mayor in Richmond has a second job — he is always the Clerk of the Market as well. On this day he has two bottles of wine handy for the first farmer to arrive at the Market Cross carrying a sample of the new crop of grain. Mind you, he can't show just any old rubbish — there's an expert on hand to make sure that it really is good quality wheat. Then there is a thanksgiving service in Holy Trinity Church and the farmer generously shares one of the bottles of wine with the Mayor and other officials.

*September 20th (Wednesday preceding)*
**St Giles's Fair**
**Barnstaple, Devon**
A special ceremony carried out at the Guildhall opens this fair. The Senior Beadle brews a special spiced ale from a secret Elizabethan recipe and this is ladled out into silver cups for those present to drink to the success of the fair.

Then toast, cheese and gingerbread and fairings are distributed. The official party then troops off to the Strand where the Town Clerk declares the fair open. A large white stuffed glove decorated with flowers and ribbons is hung over a Guildhall window as a symbol of friendship to strangers. This is a three-day fair — one day for horses, one day for horned cattle, and one day for fun (actually the fun goes on all of the time). *See* p 90.

*September 28th*
**Admission of Sheriffs**
**London: Mansion House, Guildhall**
Although you can't see the ceremony, you can see a colourful procession. From the Mansion House comes the Lord Mayor and his three household officers, senior members of the Corporation, the Aldermen and their beadles. Meanwhile the Sheriffs Elect, attended by the Liverymen of their Companies, make their way there, timing it so that they all arrive together at the Guildhall at midday.

*September 29th*
**Election of the Lord Mayor**
**London: Guildhall, Mansion House**
Now this is a ceremony which the public can go to. The reigning Lord Mayor and Sheriffs, carrying posies, walk in procession to the Guildhall and take their places on the herb-strewn dais. The Recorder directs the Liverymen to select two Aldermen and one of these is chosen by the Court of Aldermen to be the new Lord Mayor. Once the choice is made, the Lord Mayor and the Mayor Elect leave the Guildhall in the magnificent state coach for the Mansion House. This is an unbroken tradition which goes back to 1192.

*September 30th*
**Pie Powder Court**
**Bristol, Avon**
St James's Fair hasn't been held since 1838 but the Court of Pie Powder is still formally opened in the Old Market. (*See* p 91).

*September: towards the end*
**Cheese Fair**
**Frome, Somerset**
At this cheese fair the cheeses were first christened in the River Frome. Nowadays this fair coincides with the carnival week which includes an agricultural show with cheese, farm produce, animals, flowers vegetables and machinery all on display. At the end of the week there are processions and a carnival ball. *See* p 90.

*September: moveable*
**Mid Autumn Festival**
This is really a Chinese harvest festival but it is also the Moon Cake Festival because it commemorates the time when the Chinese rebelled against their Mongol overlords in the 14th century. Messages telling people of the uprising were stuck in little cakes and these were smuggled from hand to hand.

Today children stay up late and then go with their parents to the nearest hill where they light lanterns and watch the moon rise before they tuck into the traditional moon cakes and fruit.

# October

*October 6th*
**Sloe Fair**
**Chichester, Sussex**
Chichester's Fair has been held ever since 1108. It acquired its name because there used to be a sloe tree standing in Oaklands Road, the site of the fair. The pie powder court (*see* p 91) was held in the upper room of Canon Gate.

*October 10th (Monday following)*
**Pack Monday Fair**
**Sherborne, Dorset**
This fair used to start with an absolutely hideous noise. Very early in the morning young people used to parade

through the streets blowing whistles and horns, banging dustbin lids and tin cans and rattling anything that made a din.

This custom originated in 1490 when the masons working on Sherborne Abbey came to the end of their work. They packed up their tools, and led by Teddy Roe, they marched triumphantly through the streets making a great deal of noise. This so impressed itself on the townspeople that they repeated the performance whenever St Michael's Fair came round. Alas, some people made real nuisances of themselves and behaved quite idiotically, so the lively custom of starting the fair in the early morning has come to an end. *See* Charter Fairs p 90.

*October: second Wednesday*
**Goose Fair**
**Tavistock, Devon**
This used to be an important goose fair, but you are unlikely to see any geese today. This fair received its charter in 1105. *See* p 90.

*October: second Sunday*
**Harvest-of-the-Sea Thanksgiving**
**London: St Mary-at-Hill Church**
The fish merchants of Billingsgate decorate the church with fish, nets, and sometimes even with a boat. Turn up at 3 pm if you want to take part in this service.

*October 16th*
**Lion Sermon**
**London: St Katherine Cree Church**
Sir John Gayer went to Arabia on a trading expedition. Somehow he found himself alone and came face to face with a lion. He fell on his knees and prayed for help. Miraculously, the lion just gave him a sniff and padded away.

Later on Sir John became the Lord Mayor of London. He died three years later in 1649 having established a fund so that a sermon could be preached on the anniversary of his escape. If you want to hear the sermon, go along at 1.15 pm.

*October: last Thursday*
**Punkie Night**
**Hinton St George, Somerset**

As the evening draws on in Hinton St George, the village is illuminated with little bobbing lights. The children have made punkies by hollowing out mangel-wurzels and have carved them with beautiful patterns. Inside the punkies are candles. They are lit and the punkies are carried on strings and toted around the town by the children who sing the Punkie Song as they go.

*October 31st-2nd November*

**Hallowtide**
Hallowtide lasts from Hallowe'en Eve to All Souls' Day. Originally this was a Celtic festival which marked the start of the New Year. Hallowe'en fires blazed on hills to keep away witches and other evil spirits, the dead were remembered, and people tried to foretell the future. Although the church took over this festival, many of the old customs were kept up. In many places young people played mischievous tricks on neighbours, guisers performed plays, children went around with blackened faces, carrying turnip-lanterns, and young girls tried to find out what their future husband would be like. Not very many of these customs survive, but a surprisingly large number of people give Hallowe'en parties for children.

*October: moveable*
## Navaratra
This is the start of a nine day period preceding the Hindu Dashara Festival. There's singing and dancing in honour of the goddess Durga.

*October: moveable*
## Dirga Puja
This day is in honour of Sri Durga, the wife of Shiva. Families gather together and daughters in particular try to return home to see their parents.

*October: moveable*
## Dussehra
This is the tenth day of Navaratri. Visitors are welcome to join in the singing and the dancing. What Hindus are actually celebrating is the victory of King Rama. He defeated the wicked demon Ravana who had taken his wife away. He didn't manage it on his own though — the monkeys came along and gave him a hand.

Brides and engaged couples look forward to this day since it is customary for them to receive gifts from wellwishers and friends.

*October: moveable*
## Diwali
This Hindu and Sikh New Year Festival lasts for five days. Lamps are lit, houses are illuminated, and presents are distributed. The Sikhs recall that Guru Hargobind was set free after being imprisoned by a Moghul emperor.

*October: moveable*
## Rosh Hashanah
This is the Jewish New Year. It is a reminder of the creation of the world, and the blowing of a ram's horn reminds Jews of Abraham's sacrifice of a ram in place of his son. On the previous evenings apples dipped in honey are eaten to symbolise the hope of a happy new year. This is the start of a ten day period when Jews examine their consciences and consider the way which they have spent the previous twelve months.

*October: moveable*
**Feast of the Tabernacles**
This is a sort of harvest festival. It lasts for eight days and is a reminder of the wanderings of the Jews through the wilderness. Little houses are built in synagogues and gardens, and these are roofed with branches, flowers and fruit. On the seventh day of this period seven circuits of the synagogue are made with people holding palm branches, flowering myrtle and a willow branch in the right hand and a lemon in the left.

*October: moveable*
**Yom Kippur**
This is the most important day in the Jewish calendar. It is called the Day of Atonement and reminds Jews of the day when the High Priest entered the Holy of Holies in the Temple and confessed and interceded for all the Jewish people. The ceremony of Kol Nidrei assures the people that if they have been truly penitent they will be forgiven. The last service of the day depicts the closing of the gates of the Temple at nightfall. The final blowing of a ram's horn marks the end of the ten days of penitence that began with Rosh Hashanah.

*October: moveable*
**Simchath Torah**
This Jewish ceremony called the Rejoicing of the Law is a really happy occasion when the scrolls of the Law are carried in procession seven times round the synagogue with people singing and dancing.

# November

*November 5th*
**Guy Fawkes' Night**
This is the anniversary of the discovery of the gunpowder plot in 1605. A group of fanatical Roman Catholics including Guy Fawkes, Robert Catesby, Robert Winter and John

Wright believed that people of their faith, already discriminated against, were going to have an even harder time in future under King James I. They not only wanted to make sure that Roman Catholics could worship in their own way, but they wanted to see the whole of the country return to Catholicism and the only way to do it, they thought, was to get rid of king and Parliament at the same time. They took a house next door to the House of Lords and began tunnelling towards a vault beneath it. This took nearly a year but at last they broke through and stored thirty-six barrels of gunpowder in it.

They waited for the opening of Parliament when everyone of importance would be present at the same time. In the meantime Lord Mounteagle, a Catholic peer, received an anonymous letter which warned him of the plot. He went to the authorities and a search was made, but nothing was found. The conspiritors waited, excited and exhilarated — soon their moment would come. However, a second search was made and this time Guy Fawkes was found. The gunpowder was discovered, concealed behind a pile of wood. Guy Fawkes could hardly deny his guilt. He was caught red-handed with a lantern and a tinder-box. There was a hunt for his fellow conspirators and they were caught. All were tortured, tried, and executed.

Parliament decided that November 5th should be a public holiday, that bells should be pealed, cannon fired, and that special thanksgiving services should be held. Bonfires were lit, torchlight processions wound their way through towns and villages, and effigies of Guy Fawkes were burned.

Even today, just to make sure, the Houses of Parliament are still carefully searched either the evening before or on the actual morning of the State Opening of Parliament. The Yeomen of the Guard in their scarlet and gold uniforms and carrying candle-lanterns have a very careful look round to make sure that there are no conspirators or gunpowder hidden away.

*November 5th*
**Bonfire Night**
**Lewes, Sussex**
Lewes had a special reason to celebrate when the Catholic

conspirators were caught. People had not forgotten that under the Catholic Mary I seventeen local Protestants were burned at the stake as heretics.

The celebrations here are quite spectacular, and they are organized by the six Bonfire Societies. There are torchlight processions, Bonfire Boys, superb fireworks, effigies, and gigantic bonfires. Just to remind everyone what it is all about, an old 'No Popery' banner is still carried.

*November 5th*
**Bonfire Night**
**Bridgwater, Somerset**
Here you'll see a torchlight procession with a large number of illuminated floats, super fireworks including the famous Bridgwater squibs, effigies, and a stupendous bonfire.

*November 5th*
**Guy Fawkes Night**
**Edenbridge, Kent**
Go to Edenbridge to see a mammoth procession, a huge bonfire and really splendid fireworks.

*November 5th*
**Guy Fawkes Night**
**Ottery St Mary, Devon**
This is well worth watching. During the celebrations eight tar barrels are set alight and rolled down the hill. Men catch the barrels and carry them through the streets while they blaze fiercely. It's an amazing sight — it all takes place in the dark while the main bonfire blazes.

*November 5th*
**Guy Fawkes Festival**
**Rye, Sussex**
Rye has a really good celebration, but it's one with a difference since it ends with the burning of a boat.

*November 5th*
**Turning the Devil's Boulder**
**Shebbear, Devon**
No doubt the people of Shebbear enjoy a bonfire and fire-

works on this day, but there's an important ceremony to be performed first. Not far from the church is a large tree and underneath this tree is a large stone, the Devil's boulder.

The bells are rung — that's to warn any evil spirits who happen to be hovering around that they had better clear off — and then, a party of villagers led by the Vicar turn the stone. This is no easy job. Crowbars and ropes are needed to roll it over.

It seems that this boulder was dropped by the Devil and unless it is turned every year on the same day the village will prosper no longer.

*November: second Saturday*
**Lord Mayor's Procession**
**London**
This has taken place ever since 1215. The idea of this procession was to let the people of London see their new Lord Mayor as he went to swear allegiance to his sovereign. For centuries he travelled in a spendid barge down the River Thames to Westminster where the Law Courts were. In the 19th century new law courts were opened in Fleet Street and this meant that the Lord Mayor just had to make a short trip down the road so, rather than do Londoners out of their show, it was decided to make the journey to the Law Courts much longer by winding round the City of London. Today you will see a large and elaborate procession.

*November 11th*
**Firing the Fenny Poppers**
**Fenny Stratford, Buckinghamshire**
Dr Willis Brown contributed very generously towards a church and he was good at fund-raising too. He encouraged the local gentry to give generously to the church by selling space on the ceiling. Once it was yours, you could have your arms displayed on it.

The Fenny Poppers are a tribute to Dr Willis Brown. They are six miniature cannon, rather like small pots, and these are charged with 'shilling-powder' and fired with a red-hot rod at 12 am, 2 pm, and 4.15. The bangs take place in the churchyard — not the church.

*November 11th*
**Wroth Silver**
**Knightlow Hill, Warwickshire**
The Duke of Buccleigh is the Lord of the Hundred of Knightlow and so the parishes in it have to pay him his due. If you want to see this you have to get up early. Representatives of the parishes meet just before dawn on Knightlow Hill near the Knightlow Cross. A Charter of Assembly is read out, and then the Duke's agent calls upon the people to drop their money into a hollow of the Cross. Anyone who fails to do so is either fined £1 or has to present the Duke with a white bull with a red nose and red ears. Then off they all go to breakfast at Dunchurch. The Duke can't do very well out of this transaction since all he receives is from 1p to 10p from each man but he has to pay for the breakfast and for the privilege of having his own health drunk in rum and milk.

*November: fourth Tuesday*
**Courts Leet and Varon**
**Ashburton, Devon**
The Court Leet is composed of freeholders of the borough and has the right to make public 'presentments' on matters of general interest. The most amazing group of officials are elected. There is the Portreeve, rather like a Mayor, Bread Weighers, Scavengers, Pig Drivers and others, and perhaps best of all, Ale Tasters. In June these and other officials visit the taverns in the town and sample the ale. When they have decided that it is up to standard, they give the landlord a sprig of evergreen to put over his door. The Bread Weighers visit bakeries and test two loaves at each shop.

*November 30th*
**St Andrew's Day**
St Andrew, the patron saint of Scotland, had nothing to do with that country. He actually spread the Gospel in Greece and Russia until his death. He was crucified in Patras and much later his bones were taken to Amalfi in southern Italy. Legend has it that his bones were then taken to Scotland where a shrine was built. The shrine was actually covered by the cathedral of St Andrew's, Fife.

What is odd is that St Andrew's Day used to be a holiday for the lacemakers of Bedfordshire, Buckinghamshire, Northamptonshire and Hertfordshire.

*November: moveable*
**Winter Clothes for Ancestors**
The Chinese tidy up the graves of their ancestors on this day. At one time they used to cut out suits of clothes from paper, carefully address them to their ancestors, and then ceremoniously burn them at the gates of temples.

*November: moveable*
**Idil Adha**
This is a Muslim festival which lasts for four days. There are prayers at the mosque and sacrifices are made, and meat is distributed to the poor.

*November: moveable*
**Guru Nanak's Birthday**
This is the day when Sikhs remember the birthday and the life of their first Guru, the founder of their religion.

# December

*December 21st*
**Candle Auction**
**Old Bolingbroke, Lincolnshire**
Poor Folks Close is a piece of land. The rent from this provides money for an old charity. The auctioneer sticks a pin into the candle and lights the wick, and then accepts bids. When the flame reaches the pin, it drops from the candle and the person who made the final bid rents the land for the next year.

*December 24th*
**Tolling the Devil's Knell**
**Dewsbury, Yorkshire**
The bell-ringers at the parish church roll up their sleeves on

Christmas Eve and prepare for a mammoth task. First they toll the bell sixteen times by ringing it four times in sets of four, and then they toll it once for each year that has passed since the birth of Jesus. So, in 1981 it will be tolled one thousand nine hundred and eighty one times. It is said that if this custom is not observed the Devil will have a free hand in Dewsbury in the coming year, and no one wants to risk that sort of bad luck.

*December 25th*

## Christmas

Christmas is the day on which Christians celebrate the birth of Jesus Christ. December 25th wasn't chosen at random; early Christian reformers wanted to replace a pagan festival that took place at that time, but many of the pagan customs survive. Holly was supposed to be especially lucky for men. It was thought to cure people with fevers and rheumatism. Many people think it is an important evergreen because it reminds Christians of the crown of thorns that Jesus wore when he was crucified while the berries are reminiscent of the drops of blood on his forehead.

Mistletoe was considered sacred by pagans who believed it had miraculous powers and could cure all sorts of illnesses as well as protecting them from evil and bringing good luck. Because of this superstition you will never see mistletoe in a church today, but in medieval times it was placed on the altars of York Minster and the Collegiate Church at Wolverhampton.

*December 25th*
### Christmas Presents
The custom of giving Christmas presents goes back beyond the Christian era. This was the time of year when the people of Rome gave gifts to each other, and each gift had a special meaning. Honey, for example, brought a sweet and peaceful year, money brought prosperity, and candles or oil lamps meant a year full of light and happiness. Christians started giving each other presents as a reminder of the gifts brought by the Three Wise Men to the baby Jesus.

*December 25th*
**Yule Candle**
This is a custom which has completely died out. A yule candle was very large indeed, it was often coloured red or green, and it was decorated with evergreens. The head of the family lit it either on Christmas Eve or Christmas Day and it had to be kept burning until everyone went to bed. The flame was put out, but it was considered unlucky to blow it out. The lighting and extinguishing of the candle went on throughout the twelve days of Christmas. Any of the candle that remained after January 6th was carefully put away for it was a protection against evil.

*December 25th*
**Yule Log**
The yule log was an important part of the Christmas ritual. It was cut down, decorated with greenery, brought into the house, and set alight. Once it was blazing, it had to be kept burning for the twelve days of Christmas. If it went out then bad luck would enter the house. If any of log was left by January 6th, this was carefully stored so that the following year's yule log could be kindled from the wood of the old yule log. In some areas of the country cider or ale was thrown over the log just before it was set alight.

*December 25th*
**Father Christmas**

Father Christmas originated as St Nicholas, a much-loved bishop who lived in Myra in Asia Minor in the 4th century. He loved both poor people and children. He was a generous man who tried to keep his good deeds quiet. This is why the bringer of Christmas gifts is supposed to come quietly at night. St Nicholas died on December 6th, and in some countries children discover their Christmas presents on December 5th, the eve of his festival. As a bishop, St Nicholas wore splendid robes and he had a mitre on his head. So, this kindly bishop has become transformed into the jolly red-robed and hooded Father Christmas many children know so well.

*December 26th*
**Boxing Day**
Boxing Day is St Stephen's Day, December 26th. No one is quite sure just how the name came into being, but some people believe it is because it was on this day that alms boxes were opened in churches and the money distributed to the poor. In some districts this was called Stephening.

*December 26th*
**Marshfield Mummers**
**Marshfield, Avon**
If you want to see a curious collection of characters including King William, Little Man, Saucy Jack and Tenpenny Nit, then go to Marshfield at 11 am. First you will see a procession of players covered in strips of paper. These are led by the Town Crier with his bell. Then you can settle down and see this short traditional play in which Little Man is killed by King William before being miraculously brought back to life by Doctor Phinex just in time for a song and a dance. *See* Mummers' Plays, p 92.

*December 26th*
**Crookham Mummers**
**Crookham Village, Hampshire**
The Crookham Mummers' play concerns King George who fights and kills both Bold Slasher and Bold Roamer. They are brought back to life by the Doctor. The King, obviously a man of tremendous energy, also defeats the wicked

Turkish Knight, but generously tells him to clear off instead of killing him. Then there's an extraordinary duel between Father Christmas who wields a broomstick, and Johnny Jack who has a sword. Alas, Father Christmas is slain but, oddly enough, he is not resurrected.

Go along to the Chequers or the Black Horse at about midday to see this curious play. See page 92.

*December 31st*
**Fireballs**
**Stonehaven, Grampian**
Only the most skilled can take part in this custom. The fire balls consist of inflammable material soaked in tar or paraffin and stuffed into wire netting containers. As the clock strikes midnight they are lit and people swing these blazing balls of fire round and round on long pieces of wire. These whirling, flaming discs, which look absolutely spectacular, are supposed to keep away any evil spirits that may be hovering near.

*December 31st*
**Flaming Barrels**
**Allendale, Northumberland**
You'll see guisers going round the streets from about 8.30 pm onwards while people gather in the square round a large bonfire.

Then, as midnight draws near, a procession of guisers appears, each man carrying a blazing half-barrel filled with tar and other inflammable material on his head. It really is an amazing sight as each walks round the bonfire and hurls his flaming barrel onto it.

*December 31st*
**Burning out the Old Year**
**Biggar, Strathclyde**
If you are keen on red herrings, then come to Biggar. The bonfire is prepared a long time in advance and then, just before midnight, it is lit. Red herrings are toasted and eaten, the last note of midnight brings an enthusiastic rendering of Auld Lang Syne, and then young people set about their mischief — taking gates off hinges, and so on.

*December: moveable*
## Hanukkah
The evening of this day marks the start of an eight day Jewish festival which commemorates the cleansing of the Temple in 165 BC following its recapture from the Greeks. The festival lasts this length of time because when the Jews began the cleaning-up operations they found enough oil to keep their sacred light burning for eight days. Jewish children love Hanukkah — it's a time for presents and parties.

*December: moveable*
## Aashoora
This is when Muslims commemorate the death of Iman Husan, the grandson of the Caliph Ali.

*December: moveable*
## Islamic New Year
Muslims date their New Year from the time when the Prophet Muhammad left Mecca to go to Medina in AD622. It was there that he formed a religious community. Muslims remember the occasion by telling stories about the Prophet and his followers.

*December: moveable*
## Guru Teigh Bahadur's Martyrdom
The Moghul Emperor Aurangzeb had the ninth Guru beheaded in 1675. Sikhs remember his matryrdom on this day.

*December 31st*
## Joya no Kare
108 peals of bells are rung at Hindu and Shinto temples to drive away evil before the new year begins.

# Notes

**Beating the Bounds and Common Riding**
In the days when there weren't many maps it was important for local people to remember exactly where the parish boundaries ran. Once a year, usually on Ascension Day, all the villagers turned out to walk round the boundaries, and so that young people, in particular, should not forget the boundary marks, they had these well impressed upon them — they were bumped on rocks, thrown into streams and ponds, dragged through hedges and over walls, and even made to climb over the roofs of houses that were built on the boundary line.

Sometimes the beating of the bounds was done on horseback, and this was called Common Riding.

**Charter Fairs**
Life was very hard in the Middle Ages. The work was tough — no machines then — many people died young, there was no comfort at home, they were usually very poor, and so, you see, life was fairly dreary. You can imagine how they looked forward to a holy day. Every church is dedicated to a saint, so when that saint's day came round, the people of the parish had a holy day. Since religion was very important to them, they went to Mass in the morning, but the rest of the day was given up to dancing, singing, games and competitions. There was trading too, for when so many people were gathered together it was good opportunity to buy and sell.

As time went on, trading became very important in some places, so towns and villages applied for a charter from the King, just to make their fair legal. Frequently these charters were given to religious establishments like monasteries or colleges, or to landowners or the nobility. This increased their wealth since they could charge stallholders rent.

In 1331 these authorities were granted another privilege. They were allowed to decide just how long these fairs were to last. Perhaps the Bishop of Winchester was particularly greedy — he kept on extending his until it lasted twenty-four days. That wasn't a record, though. St Ives in Huntingdonshire had a fair that went on for forty days.

Pedlars used to travel from one fair to another, and as you can imagine, they became pretty dusty as they plodded from place to place. *Pieds poudreux* they were called — dusty-footed. Well, those running the fairs also had the right to set up special courts, and these became known as Courts of Pie Powder — you can see where Pie Powder came from, can't you?

These courts were necessary. Once you got large crowds, then you were bound to get brawls and quarrels too. Some people were just drunk and noisy, others complained about dishonest traders, and traders complained about awkward customers. No doubt there was petty crime too — it must have been a pickpocket's paradise. The Courts of Pie Powder heard disputes and punished offenders, often sentencing them to the stocks or pillories. These were wooden frameworks with holes in them into which the offender's arms, legs or heads were thrust. There they were stuck while the crowd hurled rotten fruit and vegetables at them. Bristol no longer has its fair, but it does still have its Court of Pie Powder.

Actually charter fairs are the only real fairs. Others should be called wakes or feasts unless they are hiring fairs. See below.

## Hiring Fairs

These fairs were established to bring employers and employees together long before we had Job Centres. They were sometimes called Mop Fairs, and magistrates decided the rates of pay and the conditions of work. Usually agreements between masters and servants lasted for a year, and so if they wanted a change, they turned up at one of these fairs. The servants gathered together in groups, each carrying a token of their skill. Shepherds carried crooks or wore a piece of sheep's wool in their hats, carters clutched their whips, milkmaids held milking pails or wore a tuft of cowhair, maids held mops, and so on.

Once the master and the servant had come to an agreement about the job, the employer handed his new employee a 'fastenpenny', and this coin was a token of wages to come. For those who failed to get a job or for either employer or servant who had changed his mind, a Runaway Mop Fair was held a little later on to give them a second chance.

## The Lunar Calendar
The moon, the only natural satellite of the earth, has a revolution of 27½ days. During this period, as far as people on earth are concerned, it seems to go from new to full. There are approximately thirteen moons in every year. Since so many religious festivals are calculated according to the phases of the moon, this explains why they are indeed moveable — they don't fall on the same calendar day each year.

## Mummers' Plays
Most mummers' plays are performed at Christmas, Hallowe'en or on All Souls' Eve, but a few, like the Pace-Egg Play, are acted at other times of the year. Very often the actors have blackened faces so that they won't be recognized, and their costumes vary from ordinary clothes decorated with long streamers of paper to quite elaborate ones. The characters vary too. The hero is sometimes St George, King George, Robin Hood or some other folk character. The villains, who are always defeated, also have a variety of names like Bold Slasher, and they are often described as Moors. There will be a fool of some sort, a Doctor, and often a Betty who is actually a man dressed up as a woman. Occasionally there is a Hobby-horse as well.

Sometimes the actors are accompanied by Morris dancers, and sometimes by Sword dancers. Where Sword dancers take part, they eventually lock their swords together round the neck of the fool. At a signal they remove their swords from the lock and the Fool falls dead. Luckily the Doctor isn't far away and he restores the Fool to life.

There are lots of variations. The King might be the restorer of life, or it could be the Betty who uses her broom to revive the Fool, but whatever they are, the intention is the same. Death is defeated. Many people think that these plays replaced the pagan practice of human sacrifice, but no one really knows their origin.

## The Muslim Calendar
The Muslim calendar dates from AD 622, when the Muslim

faith was founded. The prophet Mohammad journeyed from Mecca to Medina, where he and his friends formed themselves into a religious community.

### The Old Calendar
In 46 BC Julius Caesar introduced a year of 365 days and added an extra day every fourth year — our Leap Year. But he believed a solar year lasted 365 days and 6 hours. Actually, a solar year is 365 days, 5 hours, 48 minutes and 46 seconds. In time everyone was convinced that this was a correct measure, and in 1751 Britain came round to accepting it, but by this time the error had amounted to eleven days. So it was decided that the day following 2 September 1752 should become 14 September 1752. This led to riots, with mobs on the streets yelling and screaming, and shouting "Give us back our eleven days!" In spite of their protests, Britain finally came in line.

### Rush-bearing and Rush-strewing
Most church floors used to be made of beaten earth although some were flagged with stone. It was very chilly and uncomfortable, and so rushes were strewn on the floor to keep out the damp and the cold. This makeshift carpet used to be renewed now and again. All of the parish took part in collecting rushes. Sometimes they were carried in bundles, sometimes brought in carts pulled by specially groomed horses. This became more and more of an occasion. Morris dancers joined the procession, and children and young people carried garlands which were later hung in the church.

Gradually, though, wooden floors were introduced into churches and so the rushes were no longer needed. But in a few places traditional rushbearing still takes place.

### Well Dressing
In pagan times springs and rivers were worshipped. Everyone needed water to live so that was a good reason for venerating them. What was more, they were almost certainly the home of spirits. Wells were honoured with special ceremonies and on these occasions they were decorated.

When Christianity came to Britain the worship of both water and its spirits was forbidden, so the wells were dedicated to the Blessed Virgin Mary or to a saint. That meant that the age-old custom of dressing them with flowers and greenery and going in procession to them was acceptable because it was honouring a Christian saint and not some pagan spirit.

No one really knows the origin of well-dressing in Derbyshire but with only occasional lapses it is something that has gone on for very many years. Until about two hundred years ago the wells were just dressed with attractive garlands. Now boards are cut out and these are covered with moist clay on which flowers, leaves and berries are stuck. These pictures have become very elaborate. Often the designs are of a religious nature and they are made on the clay with a kind of mosaic consisting of flower petals, leaves, cones, berries, shells, mosses, bark and pebbles — in fact, almost any natural material is used, and the results really have to be seen to be believed.

# Index

Aashoora 89
Abbots Bromley, Staffordshire 70-1
Abbotsbury, Dorset 35
Abingdon, Oxfordshire 53
Abinger Common Medieval Fair 52-3
Abinger, Surrey 52-3
Admiralty Court 64
Admission of Sheriffs, 74
All Souls' Day 69-70
Allendale, Northumberland 88
Alnwick, Northumberland 14
Ambleside, Cumbria 62-3
Ascension Day 46
Ashbourne, Derbyshire 14-15
Ashburton, Devon 83
Aston-on-Clun, Shropshire 37-8
Atherstone, Warwickshire 15

Bacup, Lancashire 25
Baisakhi 30
Ballycastle, Co Antrim 68
Bampton, Oxfordshire 44
Barlow, Derbyshire 66
Barnstaple, Devon 73-4
Barrington Dole 24
Bartle's Burning 68
Bartlemas Day 67
Battle of the Boyne Celebrations 60
Beating the Bounds 35, 47-8, 90
Beating the Retreat 41
Beltane Festival 57-8
Berwick upon Tweed, Northumberland 33, 62
Biddenden Dole 25-6
Biddenden, Kent 25-6
Bideford, Devon 49-50
Biggar, Strathclyde 88
Birdlip, Gloucestershire 42
Blessing of Throats 11
Blessing the Nets 12
Blessing the Sea 46
Blidworth, Nottingham 9-10
Bonfire Night 80-1
Bourne, Lincolnshire 27
Boxing Day 87
Braw Lads Gathering 56-7
Bread Dole 9
Bridgewater, Somerset 81
Brigg, Humberside 65
Bristol, Avon 43, 74
Britannia Coconut Dancers 25
Bubble Sermon 49

Burghead, Grampian 5
Burning of Judas 24
Burning out the Old Year 88
Burning the Clavie 5
Burry Man and Ferry Fair 59
Bury St Edmund's, Suffolk 4
Butterworth Charity 23-4
Buxton, Derbyshire 55

Candle Auction 84
Candlemas 8
Carhampton, Somerset 5-6
Castleton, Derbyshire 39-40
Charing, Kent 41
Charles I, commemoration of death 6
Charles II, ceremonies commemorating his return from exile 39-40
Charlton-on-Otmoor, Oxfordshire 32
Charter Fairs 90-1
Cheese Fair 75
Cheese Rolling 42
Chichester, Sussex 75
Chinese New Year 2
Ching Ming 29
Christmas 85-7
Cilgerran, Dyfed 67
Cleiking the Devil 61
Clipping the Church 73
Clock Race 49-50
Coal Carrying Championship 26
Colchester, Essex 70
Commemoration of the death of Charles I 6
1346 Commemoration Service 38
Common Riding 50-1, 90
Common Walk 37
Coracle Racing 67
Corby, Northamptonshire 45
Corby Pole Fair 45
Corfe Castle, Dorset 14
Courts Leet and Varon 83
Crab Fair 73
Cranham, Gloucestershire 66
Crookham Mummers 87-8
Crookham Village, Hampshire 87-8
Cutting of the Baddeley Cake 2

Deer Roasting 66
Dewsbury, Yorkshire 84-5
Dicing for Bibles 44
Dicing for the Maids' Money 7
Dirga Puja 78

95

Distribution of Bread and Cheese 44
Diwali 78
Dressing the Arbor Tree 37-8
**Duns, Borders** 58
**Dunstable Downs, Bedfordshire** 22
**Durham** 38
Dussehra 78

East Land Auction 42-3
Easter 24-8
**Eastgate, Lincolnshire** 42-3
**Ebernoe, Sussex** 62
**Edenbridge, Kent** 81
Egg-Shackling 17
**Egremont, Cumbria** 73
Election of Sheriffs 55
Election of the Lord Mayor 74
**Eyam, Derbyshire** 69

Father Christmas 86-7
Feast of the Tabernacles 79
Feast of Weeks 48-9
**Fenny Stratford, Buckinghamshire** 82
**Findon, Sussex** 72
Fireballs 88
Firing the Fenny Poppers 82
First-footing 1
First Fruit Ceremony 73
Flaming Barrels 88
Forty Shilling Day 8-9
Founder's Day (Royal Hospital) 39
**Frome, Somerset** 75
Furry Dance 34-5

**Galashiels, Borders** 56-7
Garland Day 35
Garland Dressing 32
Garland King 39-40
Gawthorpe Feast 33-4
**Gawthorpe, West Yorkshire** 33-4
**Goathland Village, North Yorkshire** 4
Goose Fair 76
**Grasmere, Cumbria** 65
Great Fair 72
Greenhill Bower
 and Court of Array 45-6
Grimaldi Commemoration Service 19
Grovely Forest Rights 38-9
**Guildford, Surrey** 7
Guru Gobind Singh's Birthday 7-8
Guru Nanak's Birthday 84
Guru Teigh Bahadur's Martyrdom 89
Guy Fawkes' Night 79-81

**Hallaton, Leicestershire** 26
Hallowtide 77

Handball 9
Hanukkah 89
Hare-Pie Scramble
 and Bottle Kicking 26
Harvest-of-the-Sea Thanksgiving 76
**Hastings, East Sussex** 46
**Hawick, Borders** 50-1
**Haworth, West Yorkshire** 52
**Haxey, Lincolnshire** 3
**Helston, Cornwall** 34-5
**Hereford, Hereford and Worcester** 34
**High Wycombe, Buckinghamshire** 36
**Hinton St George, Somerset** 77
Hiring Fairs 72, 91-3
Hobby-Horse 32-3
Hocktide Tutti-men 27-8
**Holsworthy, Devon** 59
**Honiton, Devon** 60
Honiton Fair 60
**Hope, Derbyshire** 57
Horn Dance 70-1
Horn Fair 62, 65
Horse Fair 65
Hot Cross Buns 22
**Hungerford, Berkshire** 27-8
Hurling the Silver Ball 11

**Ickwell, Bedfordshire** 37
Idil Adha 84
**Ideford, Devon** 24
Idil Fitri 70
**Innerleithen, Borders** 61
**Irvine, Strathclyde** 69
Islamic New Year 89
Isra'Wal Mi'raj 48

Janam Ashtami 70
Jankyn Smith's Dole 4
**Jedburgh, Borders** 9
John Stow Commemoration Service 28-9
Joya no Kare 89

**Kidderminster, Hereford
 and Worcester** 53-4
King's Lynn Fair 12-13
**King's Lynn, Norfolk** 12-13
**Kingsteignton, Devon** 44-5
Kipling Cotes Derby 20
**Knightlow Hill, Warwickshire** 83
Knill Games, The 61-2

Lailatul Bara'ah 59
Lammas Fair 68
**Lanark, Strathclyde** 18
**Laugharne, Dyfed** 37
**Lerwick, Shetland** 7

Lewes, Sussex 80
Lichfield, Staffordshire 45-6, 48, 71
Lilies and Roses Ceremony 36-7
Lion Sermon 76
Little Edith's Treat 60
Liverpool, Merseyside 24
London 2, 3, 6, 11, 13, 17, 19, 21-2, 23-4, 28-9, 30, 31, 36-7, 39, 41, 47-8, 49, 52, 55-6, 63-4, 68-9, 74, 76, 82
Londonderry, Co Antrim 66-7
Lord Leycester Hospital's Celebration 40
Lord Mayor's Procession 82
Lunar Calendar 92

Marbles Championship 23
Marhamchurch, Cornwall 66
Marhamchurch Revels 66
Marshfield, Avon 87
Marshfield Mummers 87
Marymass Fair 69
Maundy Money Service 21-2
May Day 31-2
May Morning Ceremony 33
Mayor of Ock Street 53
Mayoring Day 36, 41
Maypole Dancing 37
Mid Autumn Festival 75
Midgeley, West Yorkshire 23
Midsummer Eve Bonfire 54, 58
Minehead, Somerset 32
Mitcham Fair 67
Mitcham, Surrey 67
Mop Fairs 72
Morris Dancers 44
Morris Thanksgiving 41
Mourne, Co Down 49
Mourne Wall Walk 49
Mummers' Plays 87-8, 92
Muslim Calendar 92-3


Navaratra 78
Newbiggin-by-the-Sea, Northumberland 35
Northam-on-Tweed, Northumberland 12
Northampton, Northamptonshire 40

Oak-Apple Day 39
Old Bolingbroke, Lincolnshire 84
Old Calendar 93
Olney, Buckinghamshire 16
Opening of the Oyster Season 70
Orange Rolling 22
Oranges and Lemons Service 21

Ossett, West Yorkshire 26
Ottery St Mary, Devon 81
Oxford, Oxfordshire 33

Pace-Egg Play 23
Pace-Egging 27
Pack Monday Fair 75-6
Padstow, Cornwall 32-3
Painswick, Gloucestershire 73
Pancake Day Race 16
Pancake Greaze 17
Passover 29-30
Peace and Good Neighbourhood Dinner 53-4
Peebles, Borders 57-8
Piddinghoe, East Sussex 60
Pie Powder Court 74
Plague Sunday 69
Planting the Penny Hedge 46-7
Plough Monday 4
Plough Stots Service 4
Portobello West Indian Carnival 68-9
Presentation of Knollys Rose 55-6
Preston, Lancashire 27
Pretty Maid Ceremony 59
Primrose Day Ceremony 30
Prophet Muhammad's Birthday 10
Punkie Night 77

Rakshabandhan 64
Ram Navmi 19
Ram Roasting Fair 44-5
Ramadan 63
Ratha Yatra 49
Reiver's Week 58
Relief of 'Derry Celebrations 66
Remembrance Day (Charles II) 40
Richmond, Yorkshire 73
Riding of the Bounds 33
Ripon, North Yorkshire 63
Roadwater, Somerset 6
Rochester, Kent 64
Rocking Ceremony 9-10
Rogationtide 46
Rosh Hashanah 78
Royal Epiphany 3
Royal Hospital, Bridewell 19
Royal National Eisteddfod of Wales 65-6
Running Auction 27
Rush-bearing 52, 56, 62-3, 65, 93
Rush-strewing 43, 93
Russian Orthodox Christmas 5
Rye, Sussex 41, 81

St Andrew's Day 83-4

St Briavels, Gloucestershire 44
St Cleer, Cornwall 54-5
St Columb Major, St Columb Minor, Cornwall 15-16
St David's Day 18
St Ethelbert's Fair 34
St George's Day 30
St Giles's Fair 73-4
St Ives, Cornwall 11, 44, 61-2
St John's, Isle of Man 59
St Patrick's Day 19-20
St Valentine's Day 11-12
St Wilfred's Fair 63
Samuel Pepys' Day 37
Sandwich, Kent 36, 67
Scarborough, North Yorkshire 17
Scarva, Co Down 60
Sedgefield, Co Durham 15
Selkirk, Borders 50
Shakespeare's Birthday Celebrations 30-1
Sham Fight 60
Shebbear, Devon 81-2
Sherborne, Dorset 75-6
Sheriff's Ride 71
Shrovetide 13-17
Shrovetide Football 14-16
Simchath Torah 79
Sir John Cass Service 13
Skipping 17
Sloe Fair 75
South Dalton, Humberside 20
South Queensferry, Lothian 59
Spalding, Lincolnshire 35-6
Spring Flower Parade 35-6
Sri Ramakrishna's Birthday 13
Stoke Gregory, Somerset 17
Stonehaven, Grampian 88
Stowell Court Auction 29
Stow-on-the-Wold Fair 35
Stow-on-the-Wold, Gloucestershire 35
Stratford Mop Fair 72
Stratford-upon-Avon, Warwickshire 30, 72
Swami Vivekananda's Birthday 6
Swan Upping 63-4

Tatworth, Somerset 29
Tavistock, Devon 76
Tetbury, Gloucestershire 42

Thanksgiving (Royal Hospital, Bridewell) 19
Throwing the Hood 3
Tichborne Dole 20-1
Tichborne, Hampshire 20
Tinsley Green, West Sussex 23
Tissington, Derbyshire 48
Tolling the Devil's Knell 84-5
Trooping of the Colour 52
Tu B'shvat 10
Turning the Devil's Boulder 81-2
Tweedmouth Feast Week 62
Tyburn Walk 31
Tynwald Ceremony 59

Up-Helly-Aa 7

Wake and Well Dressing 57
Warcop, Cumbria 56
Warwick 40, 72
Warwick Mop Fair 72
Wassailing the Apple Tree 5, 6
Weighing the Mayor 36
Well Dressing 44, 48, 55, 66, 93-4
West Linton, Borders 51
West Wilton, North Yorkshire 68
Whalton, Northumberland 58
Whipman's Festival 51
Whitby, North Yorkshire 46-7
Whitsun 43-7
Whuppity Scoorie 18
Widecombe, Devon 71-2
Widecombe Fair 71-2
Wingrave, Buckinghamshire 56
Winter Clothes for Ancestors 85
Wirksworth, Derbyshire 44
Wishford Magna, Wiltshire 38-9
Witch's Bonfire, The 54-5
Wool Race 42
Worcester, Hereford and Worcester 40-1
Worcester Royalist Day 40-1
Worshipful Company of Stationers' Service 17-18
Wotton, Surrey 8-9
Wroth Silver 83

Yom Kippur 79
Yule Candle 86
Yule Log 86

SC10